Women of Afghanistan

As part of our commitment to world literature, Ruminator Books is proud to offer the following additional titles in translation:

An Algerian Childhood:
A Collection of Autobiographical Narratives
 edited by Leïla Sebbar

The Belt
 by Ahmed Abodehman

The Last Summer of Reason
 by Tahar Djaout

The Watchers
 by Tahar Djaout

Women of
Afghanistan

Isabelle Delloye

TRANSLATED FROM THE FRENCH BY
Marjolijn de Jager

Foreword by André Velter

Ruminator Books
SAINT PAUL, MINNESOTA

Copyright 2003 by Ruminator Books

Published by Ruminator Books
1648 Grand Avenue
St. Paul, Minnesota 55105
www.ruminator.com

First Ruminator Books printing 2003

Originally published as *Femmes d'Afghanistan*
Copyright 2002 Éditions Phébus, Paris

Dust jacket design by Krista Olson
Book design by Wendy Holdman
Typesetting by Stanton Publication Services, St. Paul, Minnesota

Printed in Canada

10 9 8 7 6 5 4 3 2 1

Library of Congress Cataloging-in-Publication Data

Delloye, Isabelle.
    [Femmes d'Afghanistan. English]
    Women of Afghanistan / Isabelle Delloye ; translated from the
French by Marjolijn de Jager ; foreword by André Velter.
        p.   cm.
    Translation of: Des femmes d'Afghanistan.
    Includes bibliographical references.
    ISBN 1-886913-59-5
    1. Women—Afghanistan—Social conditions.   I. Title.
    HQ1735.6.D4413 2003
    305.42'09581—dc21

                                                    2003004047

For Laïli, Waïda, Shirîn, Trina, Begom, Mina,
Zarmina, Roshana, Nour, Sêma, Helaï, Faôzia,
Aziza, Nazanîn, Rouia, Mâghal, Anahita, Latifa,
Zarlasht, Breshna, Malalaï, Soraya, Touba, Zohra,
Wagma, and Rushana—my Afghan sisters of every
ethnicity and every social class.

For Salaouddine Ghazi, Gholam Sakhi, Sher,
Shoukour, Nadjib, Walid, and Zalmaï, for Mirdad,
and for my friend Homayoun, a careful reader.

That red on the horizon is not the dawn's
For my sighs have ignited the sky.

(Pashto *landay*)

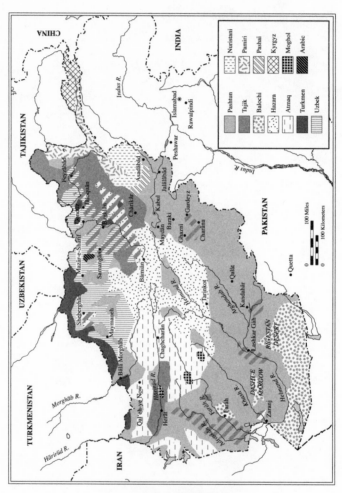

AFGHANISTAN
ETHNIC GROUPS

Contents

Foreword

Lifting the Veil

André Velter

Perhaps Afghanistan is coming out of a long night. A twenty-three-year ordeal combining several wars and every possible atrocity—coup d'état, invasion, war of liberation, civil war, vengeance in various forms, barbaric acts, torture, summary executions, and holy wars changed into dirty wars, have left a country in ruins, a people traumatized, minds in confusion, and a way of life that has been lost.

But at the heart of this night an even darker region existed, still unknown, still ignored, still muzzled, and sometimes murdered. A region that came from a far greater distance, lay anchored at a much greater depth. A region of oppression bequeathed to generation after generation like a cruel and cursed inheritance. A region where another form of immutable and secret war prevailed.

Little girls, daughters, wives, mothers, widows, grandmothers—those who hold up half the sky, as once was said elsewhere—were kept in submission here, moved under surveillance from one residence to another, if not in a household prison under the successive or joint control of a father, brother, husband, or son. Except for the aristocracy, intellectuals, and a handful of progressive activists, nobody was concerned about a situation that, as it increased its prohibitions and bullying, more than resembled a pure and simple state of servitude.

Unless one wants at all costs to define a situation unconditionally and without any awareness, there is no real question here of

women's status. The "second sex" did not exist. The only concern
was to be assured of procreation and work: reproduce and produce.
Any and all ideas of autonomy, emancipation, desire, or awakening
were taboo, repressed, and dangerous. Women had a function but
no destiny, unless it was taking the deadly risk of challenging the
customary order that combines the male code of honor and Islamic
law so as to increase the subjugation.

The coming to power of the Taliban in 1996 would, to the point
of caricature, codify the position that excluded from the world and
almost from life the very ones for whom no other right was recognized than that of giving birth. It will always be relevant to remember that the destruction of this abject regime occurred only after it
suffered peripheral assaults and huge collateral damages, but that
destruction most certainly did not have the goal of putting an end
to the suffering of Afghan women.

The first virtue of the book you are about to read is that it breaks
a vast silence. It is an attempt to forcefully open a door meant to be
seen by everyone: the men of Afghanistan and from everywhere else,
including those who, in their fascination with this sumptuous country of ancient traditions, hardly dwell on its massive dark shadow.
Women, too, are affected by what they might hear, in the diversity of
their own voices, which constitutes their common fate as much as it
individualizes them. Above all, they may measure the extent to which
the social and religious game, said to be sacrosanct, traps them and
then forces them to accept and legitimize this same trap.

A single reply sometimes opens onto chasms of frustration,
contradictory affection, and finally definitive submission. One example: Adela, twenty-three years old, taken as the second wife of a
soldier when she was twelve, already the mother of four, answers the
question, "Are you satisfied with your life?" by stating simply, "I am
satisfied with my children."

Dialogues such as these, in a minimum of words, take on the
weight of all the grief that cannot be spoken. And therein lies the

other virtue of this book that, in defiance of any "literature," frequently creates these blinding sparks with restraint of expression or with bits and pieces seized from an oppressing muteness. Keeping everything in proportion, a carefully attentive, affectionate, and discreet listener, Isabelle Delloye has organized and transcribed the words as closely as possible and thus they are kindred to the strongest pages of Sadeq Hedayat, the great Iranian writer, who uses a raw and coarse, almost savage realism to chronicle his explorations of human suffering.

Publisher's Note

(from the French edition)

Film director and editor in her spare time, bookstore owner and publisher for a while, designer, creator, and installer of ceramic tiles used in architecture (Paris, San Francisco, Berkeley, Brooklyn, and New York), and always a traveler, Isabelle Delloye has lived and worked in Afghanistan, Tunisia, Nicaragua, Pakistan, and the United States; she currently resides in Paris.

For four years (1974–1978), Delloye lived in Kabul, where she taught at the Lycée Français. She returned to France in 1980 with *Women of Afghanistan,* which has been considered a classic ever since its initial publication by Éditions des Femmes. Delloye wanted to revise the book completely last spring when the Taliban, under the generally indifferent eyes of the rest of the world, destroyed the mythical giant Buddha statues of Bamiyan. Little did she know that Afghanistan would soon and so tragically be back in the spotlight.

The reason Delloye wanted to rework her book—adding other, more up-to-date documentation and, in the fall of 2001, revising her Introduction in light of the most recent events—was that in the twenty years since she had shown the troubled humanity of Afghanistan working and struggling, their wounds had not healed. In fact, their injuries had become deeper and more acute. Expanding her book, as she decided to do now exactly a year ago, had become a kind of moral obligation for Delloye. For it is certain—as reading the following pages will confirm—that, even after she herself was forced to leave, she never abandoned Afghanistan, and a central part of her continues to live there.

When she put this text together in the early eighties, Delloye had not wanted to write a book as much as create the opportunity for a variety of women's voices to be heard, thereby fading into the background herself as much as she could. The same discretion, rather rare in these times of deafening media noise, had already taken the critics, who were not hiding their confusion or emotion, by surprise when the first version of the book appeared. Thus in *Le Nouvel Observateur* Katia D. Kaupp could write: "With a preface, many personal accounts, some commentary, songs, and clandestine texts, *Women of Afghanistan* presents itself as a slowly unfolding tapestry in which the characters are quite naturally placed in history. An enthusiastic and unpretentious experiment, this is the opposite of journalistic exploitation. . . . With a certain grace and an open-handed naïveté, Isabelle Delloye has managed to capture the pure fragrance of Afghanistan. As putrid as it may have become, the air never smells of gunpowder and bullets alone. It smells of the Afghan people. They are all here, terribly alive on the page and between the lines, women and men, children and old people. They are so engaging in their startling way of life, which pours out like a myth with its legendary heroes . . . against a backdrop of endless horizons, horses, and enslaved women."

Twenty years later, Isabelle Delloye has remained faithful to the same observation post—that of attentive friendship voluntarily discreet, of experience noiselessly but warmly shared. And her book, if it communicates a new harvest of information, if it lets still other voices be heard, makes no greater claims than it did before. It states what was, with no further ado. It refrains from judgment but also from concealing anything.

Women of Afghanistan

Twenty Years Later: March 2001

The Taliban declare that they are going to destroy the giant statues of Buddha at Bamiyan.

A flood of memories engulfs me: the only street of this large town in the high mountains, inns heated by huge stoves set beneath the earth in the icy halo of the falling evening, the smell of wood fires, of furs spread on the ground, and the cries of children chasing chickens for the dinner of travelers who, after a long day's trek over dusty roads, have arrived from Kabul. And then the always-starry night in this high valley in central Afghanistan, the incomparable silence in the ghostly shadow of survivors of a faith that sculpted mountains. I saw them for the last time in October 1978, six months after the coup d'état that put the Communists in power in Afghanistan.

The earliest Muslim conquerors of this region are supposed to have mutilated the statues—they no longer had faces, hands, or anything that seemed to have any meaning, yet there they were and the power they exuded was undiminished. The sublime beauty, associated with the independent spirit of the region's Hazara people, undoubtedly inspired the hatred of the Taliban and validated their wish to attack these giants, who were never intended to belong to anyone. The notion of safeguarding historic monuments or humanity's heritage is an invention of the modern world, and the men in power in Kabul live in another era.

With this dramatic action they intend to provoke the countries of the West that want to impose their model on the world—models for human rights, for the reverence for historic monuments and for nature. Before, in Afghanistan, most people used to respect differences and wanted to learn from them. "Progress," in the sense of advancing toward modernity, started to be felt in the early seventies. The veil, then known as *chadri* and peculiar to Afghan cities, was the object of mockery, and women wore it less and less. Men did or did not have a beard or a mustache, did or did not wear a turban or hat, traditional Afghan dress or a city suit. The modern world and traditional customs coexisted and did not collide. This kind of balance was so exceptional that it should come as no surprise that the war, with its destruction, its killings, and its human refugees, prompted such a major regression.

One might ask whether the primary problem of Afghanistan stems from the diversity and cultural wealth of the populations that make up the country. Rare is the Westerner who has not fallen in love with this extraordinary sweep of humanity. It should be clearly recognized that those who wanted to assist the Afghans in emerging from the war have never had an easy task. Trying to differentiate between them and those defending fundamentalist Islam is a lost cause. Before this war, one would speak of "Muslim brothers" without distinction, the way one speaks of fundamentalists in Christianity or Judaism. Ahmad Shah Massoud belonged to a fundamentalist party but fought against terrorism; the positions he took were clear-cut, but nobody heard him.

If one looks far back in time, the land that is now Afghanistan has been prey to nomadic invaders from the Central Asian steppes and then acted as a buffer state, caught in a stranglehold between Russia and the British Empire in the nineteenth century. Whole regions in ruins and massacred, but also lands of superior civilization, conquered by Alexander the Great at the end of his life and becoming the point of departure for the India of the Grand Mogul Empire.

More recently, in 1973, King Zaher Shah was dethroned by his cousin Daoud Khan, who created the republic. Five years later, on

April 27, 1978, pushed to the limit by the arrest and threatened exe-
cution of their party's leaders, the Communists took power. Some
campaigns ensued in August, and centers of resistance were gaining
ground continuously. Since, despite a policy of terror, the Afghan
Communists had become powerless, the Soviets invaded the country. Then the war extended throughout the area, and regions that
had practically broken away each chose their own group, more often
than not fighting the common enemy separately. Old men were arrested, as were young girls, women and their babies, all of them as
political prisoners. The horror of mass graves was already in the air.
The population in the cities had not yet encountered the strength
of its enemy: "They won't hold out," they said. "Nobody has ever
colonized us." In appearance, there was a similar resistance to the
common foe in the name of Islam, but already some groups—such
as that of Gulbuddine Ekmatiar—were attacking other resisters,
playing a rather perverse game in order to gain control over the
areas of poppy cultivation. They would not hesitate to bomb Kabul,
after it had been taken by a coalition of Tajiks, Uzbeks, and Hazaras
when the invaders left.

In 1992, when the Communists fell, Ahmad Shah Massoud held
power. Did he attempt to bring Afghans together, to reconstruct
the country, and to provide answers to the problems of a society
that had been bled dry? Civil war raged, and he was completely
preoccupied with the defense of Kabul against the ongoing attacks
of his opponents. In 1996, the Taliban took Kabul, urged on by
the Pakistanis, who in turn were supported by the United States.
Pakistan had always worked to destabilize its neighbor to the north.
The Americans undoubtedly thought that by saluting the coming
to power of the Taliban, the latter would be indebted to them and
would serve their economic interests. There are, in fact, huge oil
reserves in Uzbekistan, and Afghanistan offers a direct route to the
Indian Ocean for possible oil pipelines. But the United States had
not foreseen that the puppets would escape them. The new masters

of Kabul then imposed laws that seemed absurd and monstrous to the modern world. One forgets that these rural Pashtun, trained in Pakistan, were for the most part born in refugee camps; for years they attended exclusively male Koranic schools, where they were raised in a singularly war-oriented atmosphere. They knew nothing about our world, which their evil genies rendered as diabolical. For them, the West was a modern form of Gog and Magog. For years, the extremists originally from Arab countries or simply from Pakistan, had come to enlarge their troops. Impious Kabul definitely had to be punished, and the city today is a field of ruins.

There have always been Taliban in Afghanistan, but they were only a small element of the society. The stronger authority was that of the elders, the wise. What was new was that the extremists had come to power—those who had been gently mocked by reasonable people proclaimed their laws that conformed to criteria and logic only they understood. Besides, without a doubt there is nothing but a series of absurd historical events to be grasped: the social injustice of the period of President Daoud Khan playing into the hands of the Communists, the Communists bringing in the Soviets, the Soviets calling for resistance, the resistance calling for fratricidal war, and the fratricidal struggles leading to acts of violence and a loss of morality.

The torpor of a decimated and exhausted population, a devastated country and economy laid the groundwork for the Taliban, who were not all that badly received by the local peoples, no matter what the West says. But the new ayatollahs seemed entirely incapable of looking ahead—they declared a return, peculiar even in Afghanistan, to social rules whose origins one could well question. And yet, we know what other countries do with human rights, countries that are UN members, such as Saudi Arabia. Women must wear the chador, and Koranic law, the sharia, is enforced with the same brutality as it is in Afghanistan. But these nations are rich, whereas Afghanistan is extremely poor and cannot manage without international aid, which it is denied because of the Taliban. Isolated from the rest of the world, the population as a whole is left behind in ignorance. Bin Laden, public enemy number one, has feathered his nest there, connected by marriage to the leader of the Taliban, the mysterious Mullah Omar.

Superimposed over the images of Afghanistan in ruins are those of the country before the war, at a time when it used to attract great travelers.

We had the good fortune to have lived there between April 1974 and December 1978. I was teaching at the Lycée Esteqlal and my husband, Emmanuel, at the university. Every weekend, every vacation we would hit the road to travel through the country, close to home or farther afield, depending on the amount of time we had available. We would load up the jeep with the whole family, accompanied by one of our Afghan students, sometimes having him discover his own country with us. After two hours on the road, we would all be covered with a layer of fine dust that had infiltrated the car. We didn't go very fast, as we would have to stop constantly to remove the biggest stones in the road, and the sometimes swollen streams had to be crossed with infinite care.

There are throngs of memories . . .

On the road north, Sharikar and its natural ice cream made in huge bowls full of snow well into the summer.

The *mantus,* small steamed pâtés we would eat in Mazar-i-Sharif[1] near the mosque with its blue ceramic dome. The stories about genies told in the evening when the lamp would start to flicker and a shiver would run through you as the supernatural was beckoned.

In Tashkurghan, breakfasts of tea, bread, and cream in the magnificent covered bazaar overflowing with marvels as in ancient Bukhara.

---

[1] The main city in the north where Ali is supposed to be buried and where the Shiites go on pilgrimages.

The horse market at Kunduz and bargaining with dealers; then returning home with the little donkey in the car, the children's arms around him.

In Herat, at the portals of Persia, birds in their cage enthralling the street and the shoemaker, who knew thousands of verses of the Persian poets Hafez or Saadi.

Our students and friends in Kabul introduced us to their families of the provinces. Zalmaï took us to Dar-i-Nur, where Bâbâ-djon and his wife, his sons, and his daughters welcomed us, proof that he accepted us into the tribe. These country gentlemen were extremely refined. Their traditional house enclosed a kind of Garden of Eden where a spring flowed and fruit trees grew. In the courtyard, the daughters were baking bread in a hole in the ground. When the father was tired, his youngest son would massage his legs, gently and without a word.

In Kapissa, land of vineyards, lived the adorable aunt of Homayun, one of my senior students at the Lycée Esteqlal. One Friday we had lunch together in the shade of a mulberry tree. The embroidered tablecloth was laid out right on the ground. It was hot and a small irrigation canal ran along the orchard. We went swimming, fully dressed, in the icy water.

Among my memories is Besmellah's dazzling smile when we brought him along to visit Bamiyan, his birthplace. Besmellah was one of the children whom Father Serge de Beaurecueil—*Warmwelcome,* so aptly named—had taken into his home in Kabul and successfully treated for tuberculosis of the bone.

Then there are the long hikes in the mountains of Badakhshan and Nuristan, to some high mountain lake, a spawning ground of giant trout.

There were the long horseback rides on the steppe behind the airport where, together with Rachid, who resembled a Joseph Kessel character, and our friend Louis, the doctor, we would train the horses we had acquired in the north, in Kunduz, to keep them in shape. We had stables built for them, in the yard right in the middle of the city. No, I can't forget the happiness—theirs and ours—in the snow that covered Kabul and its surroundings from the end of November to mid-March beneath a cloudless blue sky; their sense of play in the parodies of *buzkashi* that we used to organize during weekend outings with our friends. And the unforgettable fragrance of the flowers of the jujube trees in spring on the road near the gates of Kabul.

The enormous monitor lizards we would encounter when going for rides toward Istalif and Paghman, the ghost town that was built early in the century and modeled after the coastal towns of Normandy by King Amanullah, who loved France and wanted his country to be modernized. In Paghman, the inhabitants of Kabul would bring their picnics to the banks of the river; these were truly elaborate meals in large pots they would reheat over fires made between two stones. Cloths were spread out on the grass under the trees, and, trying not to show their legs too much, the young girls would dip the tips of their toes in the icy and crystal-clear water. This is where one could stay cool in the summer when the capital, despite its altitude, was broiling under a sweltering sun.

I remember the gigantic and superb source that comes from the mountain high above the Valley of the Kings, Dar-e-Adjar, where we went camping more than once to go trout fishing.

I also remember the site of the terraced lakes of Band-e-Amir and the only inn, like a mountain refuge where, the last time we went there, we took Nadjib and Shna, his first cousin whom he had just married in accordance with a family agreement made when he was nine years old. Married at eighteen, he was a student at the Lycée Esteqlal, soon to be on a government grant in France. She had recently arrived from the small village where she was born in the region of Jalalabad and could barely speak Persian. Today they live in the suburbs of Paris with their two sons, both born in France.

And then there is the journey to Panshir, where our horses would spend the summer in the coolness of the high mountain valleys. One night with a full moon and with Rachid as our guide, we had crossed the steppe at a regular and steady trot, singing at the top of our voices. On the way, we'd ask to be put up, and there was always a guestroom where we would be made welcome. There would be moments of mad laughter when, just as we'd begin to doze off, our host would come back ten times to ask us if we needed anything. On the way back, as we'd cross the newly harvested vineyards, the horses would forage for picked-over grapes.

Most memorable is without a doubt the solicitude with which we were received and how we were always offered the best morsels of the dish our host shared with us.

And then, when one begins to set up camp before nightfall, the Afghan desert has the strange ability to generate human beings, small boys, adolescents, or adults who come from nowhere, one by one, and sit down with you in a circle around the fire. Questions then come from every side. Often the first one is, "From what tribe are you?"

I can see Stéphane again, our little brother who used to raise falcons under the iron rule of Batshe Kâkâ, who tamed sparrow hawks, peregrine falcons, and magpies. We would bring gorgeous little quails back from the bird bazaar to feed the predatory ones.

For a time, our neighbor was Father de Beaurecueil, *padar,* a Dominican priest and Orientalist who had opened his doors to some twenty impoverished and often seriously ill young boys. One of these was Mirdad, an orphan, who came to live with us when Stéphane was in Kabul.

I remember the Pantagruelian meals that Sher, our Panshiri cook whom we called "uncle," would prepare and his delight upon my return from the maternity clinic when, holding the baby with expert hands, he paraded through the house repeating over and over again, "I told you it would be a son!"

And Laïli, who watched the children when I was working and whom I would catch turning somersaults with the baby on the carpet when I came home.

And Bâbâ, the gardener who used to have his beard trimmed stylishly on the sidewalk across the street.

The first one was a Sunni, the second an Ismaelite, and the third a Shiite, and they would have their meals in separate dishes.

Nor have I forgotten our outings to the "street of thieves," the antiques bazaar, the currency exchange bazaar, and expeditions to the animal bazaar where we'd find all the fauna of Afghanistan in a pitiful state in cages.

Evenings spent at the homes of friends who had us meet father and mother in Kabul—Khalil, Walid, Nadjib, Ashraf and Marie, Sala and Elaï, Amin, Wahid, Adela, Trina, Fahim . . . Fahim, who introduced us one day to his father's two wives and, with a little knowing smile, said in French, "My mothers!"

Afghans laugh about the same things the rest of us do, and they have a fantastic sense of humor. They love poetry, which from the earliest age they practice in school in oratorical contests. They love music and games of all kinds—pigeon flying; kite flying; the famous *buzkashi* in which two teams on horseback fight over the hide of a goat or a calf; the game of poles in which horse riders going at top speed with their long poles have turbans that unwind and float like banners; and the animal fights—cocks, dogs, rams, and partridges.

We would spend part of the nights of Ramadan listening to music in the city's restaurants, unfamiliar but delighted with the classical Indian canons.

There were also children who, as we passed by, would sing a counting song that everyone knew: "Fiend of Satan eating during Ramadan, don't eat too much or you'll explode!" Sometimes they'd throw stones, treating us like heathens. Yes, if I now evoke what I loved in Afghanistan, it is because I have forgotten its annoyances, which exist as they do everywhere. For there are devils, liars, thieves, traitors, and criminals, but no more so than anywhere else.

I am not from Afghanistan—I have a hard time telling myself where I do come from and recognizing my hometown—but I love that country, those immense spaces that industrialization has not defiled, that land of purity and impudence; and the peoples who inhabit it are part of my own.

Twenty years ago, Éditions des Femmes published a number of accounts I had collected during my stay in Afghanistan. At the time, the distribution of the book was restricted by the fact that it had immediately been labeled as a feminist and anti-Muslim treatise, which was far from the truth.

The years that have gone by since then have allowed me the distance needed to lose any subjectivity regarding the narratives I had collected, translated, and turned into a book. Rereading them has moved me deeply. I have been struck by the value they have beyond any era or politics; the voices of these often very poor women, which tell the story of Afghanistan before the war, would never have had any chance of getting out of the country. I deliberately am not using the term *disappeared* to talk about this country before the war, for I am absolutely convinced that in the Afghan countryside today people have not changed their ideals or their behavior.

In November 1985, I went to film a documentary for French television on the situation of Afghan women and children in the refugee camps in Peshawar, Pakistan.[2] There I met old men and women who told of the ordeals they had endured, and I was struck that those exiles had been able to keep intact the rules of courtesy, hospitality, humor, and vivaciousness. Later, when I had to choose a research topic for a postgraduate certificate in ethnographic cinematography, the con-

---

[2] *Femmes afghanes en exil* (Afghan Women in Exile), TF1, *Magazine Infovision,* program broadcast on January 21, 1986.

stancy of my friend Shna, a refugee living in Paris, led me to conclude that she carried her country and her culture within her. The film I produced was titled *La Maison est le monde* (Home Is the World).

Nadjib is an old friend, who in his senior year was my student at the Lycée Esteqlal in Kabul, a lycée inaugurated in 1968 by Georges Pompidou and financed by the French government. Its best students used to obtain scholarships for study at French universities. . . .

I know Shna much less well than Nadjib. . . . Her gestures fascinate me. My camera focuses on her hands, her face, and not on the food she is preparing or the objects around her. It is like her clothes, which she actually bought in France but transformed to fit her personal use, her personal fashion: she is dressed like the women of Kabul. The family is poor and they have brought nothing from their country, no carpets, no jewelry. And, as I continue filming, I understand one of the explanations for the mystery: in her home, in the apartment of one of the housing projects just outside Paris, I am in Afghanistan because Afghanistan is inside her. In her gaze, when she looks me straight in the eye, in the automatic gesture of replacing the veil that constantly slides down from her hair to her shoulders, in the way she breaks the eggs in the skillet, the air we are breathing here is air from Afghanistan.

Twenty-three years ago, my son was about to be born in Kabul. The war in Afghanistan had just begun. In the ninth month of my pregnancy, during the lightning air strike of April 24, 1978, by Soviet MIGS, we had taken refuge underneath the house in the Shor-e-Naw district, the lovely house of Bâbâ-djon, where we were living with our children and friends who might be staying with us. That particular day, there was a young doctor with us, Philippe, who had just arrived in Kabul to work abroad in lieu of doing his military

service. We were rather foolishly—if one considers the tons of
earth our house represented in case of a bombing—joking about
the fact that he had never delivered a baby before and that, in an
emergency, we'd be in trouble in this improvised cellar if he had to
cut the umbilical cord. Three weeks later, during curfew, my friend
Trina, an obstetrician, delivered me under safe conditions in the
city's women's hospital. The next day, at seven o'clock in the morning, Emmanuel brought us back home. I retain of this time the
strange sense of a cocoonlike ambience. The thrill of having a son
after our two daughters, the nights of camping when we would put
the mattresses of our two little girls on the floor in our bedroom so
that we'd be close together, the questions we had about the future of
our adopted country that had absorbed us into its unfailing friend-
ships, the hope for a more just society, and then, day by day, the
atmosphere of suspicion and a gnawing concern about the lot of
this one or that one.

Our friend Sala was arrested with his wife and son, as were all
the members of the royal family present in Kabul at the moment of
the coup d'état. Every day we were waiting to hear the news of their
liberation, when we learned of the death of our friend, an aesthete of
such immense refinement and simplicity. It was said that his tortur-
ers had demanded that he intervene in the surrender of Nuristan,
which had seceded in the first days of the Communist takeover.
Obviously, he had not given in.

He had initiated us into the delights of classical Indian music,
which he knew thoroughly, and we had frequently invited him to
the concerts we used to organize at home for our friends. Afghan
musicians such as Ustad Sarahang, Mir Mohmad, or Ustad Malang
would be here, and the most diverse people would attend—Gholam
Sakhi, the cabinetmaker, Gholam Sakhi, the hairdresser and an
equally excellent player of *retchak* (a drum with two strings and a
bow), boys from the lycée and the university, young girls from the
Kabul upper class, neighbors who were music lovers, Sher—the

cook—who having sedately removed his apron after dinner would join us informally, and guests from Europe or India who happened to be staying with us. To Sala we also owe, among other marvelous moments in our life in Afghanistan, duck and partridge hunts in the high central plateaus not far from Dasht-e-Naour.

It very quickly grew obvious that we were becoming a danger to all those who approached us, since we were not card-carrying members of the French Communist Party. Loyalty is an Afghan quality, however, and our house had always been a haven of peace for our friends of both genders and all ages, of every ethnicity and social class.

We decided to send our little girls back to France as they were a bit traumatized by the distressing atmosphere and the sporadic gunfire. In Kabul, the school year ended in late November due to the rigorous climate of the city, which is situated at an altitude of eighteen hundred meters. I could then ask for time off from the National Education Department "to raise my children," and we decided that I would go home to Paris with the baby before my husband, who was not able to break his contract before the end of the term, and that he would join us the following summer.

As the plane took off from Afghan soil, everyone was crying, myself included.

The war that was to tear up the country had stopped me right in the middle of my work recording the narratives of Afghan women. When peace still reigned, I had imagined spending time with Turkoman and Uzbek women in the north, with the Pashtun nomads of the high central plateaus, and even with the Kirghiz women, who had agreed that I could follow their seasonal migration that was to begin at Pamir. None of that was possible, but nonetheless I decided to publish the accounts I had collected as a small book in which I would bring these women's voices to the French reader. Adding a few pages of feminist documentation, Éditions des Femmes accepted my manuscript, but the mistrust that accompanied the appearance of the book in the circles of "defense of the Afghan resistance against the Soviet occupation" obscured the women's testimony. It was preferred that the delicate topic of the condition of women in Afghanistan not be broached.

It is a privilege to have been able to live in Afghanistan, a privilege for me to have been able to gather these personal accounts of women at a period when one could move about freely and speak openly in that country. It is partly to honor that debt that Emmanuel wrote *Les Bazars de Kaboul* (The Bazaars of Kabul) with André Velter. It is a book that bears witness to a place that was destroyed during the war.

The wrecking of the Buddhas of Bamiyan reminded the world of this country's dramatic situation, which everyone was beginning to forget since it no longer symbolized the struggle against communism. Thereafter it was no longer mentioned.

In March 2001, surrounded by general indifference, when people were dying of hunger and the Taliban were threatening the Buddha statues, Japan had offered staggering sums of money to save the sculptures. "Our children are dying of hunger and you are weeping over statues of stone! This is what we'll do with them!"

A barbaric and stupid destruction, was the comment made at the time by Alain de Bures, a French agronomist who had just devoted twenty years of his life to helping Afghan farmers survive. But it was just as stupid to isolate Afghanistan from the Taliban, thereby playing the extremist game and taking any chance away from the moderates who would have liked to bring their country out of the chaos.

The attacks of September 11, signed off on by Osama bin Laden, will shake the history of a people that was gradually sinking into obscurantism, but whose Taliban leaders were initiating a dialogue with the Western world.

It was a suicidal attack in all respects, since it provoked an American reaction that will bring down the Taliban regime. On November 13, 2001, the Northern Alliance quietly took Kabul. To the great joy of the people, women's voices and music were heard again and men rushed to the barber. A police force was formed to avoid trouble in the city. Quickly it was announced that women would be able to go back to work and their daughters to their studies.

Religion has always pervaded Afghan daily life, and in this society everyone knows perfectly well what is proper and what is not. Boys and girls are born and grow up according to a precise ritual. There are specific foods for every moment of life, specific games and pleasures for every celebration. Life was lived to the beat of tradition. The war ripped families apart, as it did villages and clans, but it seems that, even in exile, Afghans are intent on maintaining their tradition through the education of their children, in the relationships between men and women, and in the respect for what is and is not allowed.

In the countryside, it is likely that families—if they haven't been decimated by the war—lead pretty much the same life as before. It is in the cities that the condition of women has dramatically worsened. Even if it is only a question of 2 percent of Afghan women, it is on their shoulders that the hope rests of having the country evolve toward modernity.

Through these narratives, a whole country is depicted. It is a country that the young Afghan men and women born in exile cannot know, but also a country that will need all of their strength to begin life anew and to develop.

Woman's Place: 1980

Afghanistan, a land without women? Brightly colored silhouettes glimpsed in the fields or infrequent apparitions brushing by you in the cities' bazaars. Endless fabric, folds of material, veils with mesh-covered openings. Heavy doors and high walls hide them from indiscreet glances. But behind all of this there are women's faces. Beautiful or ugly, their fate is the same: they belong to the men. Like a garden jealously guarded by its owner against intruders, the daughter belongs to her father and her brothers before she becomes the asset of a husband. Then she is his property and he can do with her as he sees fit.

When the eye has grown refined enough to notice the infinite shades of ocher in soil and rock, it detects the thorny shrubs, the dark spots made by the tents, the unreal outlines of the camels in the burning and vibrating air. A ghostlike shadow emerges from the dust raised by a herd of sheep. The beauty of a Pashtun nomad and his son, whose faces are protected by a strip of their turban, revealing a life beyond time that challenges a modern world it does not crave. "Why are you taking a picture? What's the point?" Around the curve of the path a luminous valley appears, very green and so valuable in the aridity of the mountains, while silvery poplars stand in tight rows on the edge of the river. A group of peasants, bare to the waist, have rolled up their wide pants to move one arm of the river aside. They're urging each other on to carry the heavy stones and branches that are to fortify the irrigation canals. On the edge of the road, a man behind his plow is finishing working a field to the slow rhythm of his oxen. In the distance, spots of bright color in the shade of an orchard—young girls are collecting the fruit of a mulberry tree in a sheet they hold stretched out while a boy perched high in the foliage is shaking the branches. The village blends into the landscape—its houses are made of the beige, ocher, or brown earth all around. On a rooftop terrace, a woman is spreading fruit to dry in the sun, apricots, mulberries, or grapes. Nomads have staked their tents away from the village close to the water. Children are playing around a large tree; they have thrown a rope around the main branch, and two little girls are swinging on it as high as they can. Their skirts are flying, and their veils, coming undone in the wind, turn into long scarves.

When you come from abroad, at first all you meet are men. Early on in my stay, I was not very comfortable in the street, but you quickly learn to avoid the looks of men passing by and, as long as you are properly dressed—a scarf over your head and a long shirt over slacks—you are free to go where you want.

I was a teacher in a boys' school, and as a foreigner and privileged among women, I was admitted into circles made up entirely of men. This afforded me some very special encounters. In Nuristan, I remember a man who was on the road at the same time we were. During the long hours of walking, he quite plainly made it his task to convert me, gently arguing that chronologically the time of Jesus had been passed and I should take a step forward on the path of spirituality and embrace the Muslim faith. He had me endlessly repeat prayers in Arabic. Another day, sitting with a friend on the bank of a river near the "hot spring" that, they say, has the power to heal the sick, I was resting up from a long hike in upper Nuristan. An old man, sitting not far away with his wife, approached us, handed us bread, and then moved away again. A moment later, he rinsed the glasses they had just used and, without a word, served us boiling hot tea. I also became familiar with the sweet welcomes, the warm smiles of the one who invites you to spend the night in his house and, as you are leaving, gives you his blessing, the careful attentions of the host watching to be sure you always have everything you need. A privilege, too, to have true friends with whom you can speak of everything, sincere and loyal friends, who are curious and often naive when faced with a woman.

In the end, the confining and somewhat forced atmosphere of the male living rooms began to weigh on me. No doubt, my incongruous presence was the cause. All the more so because the whispering, the stifled noises, and the bursts of laughter coming from the pantries always ended up penetrating the walls of the guest room.

I finally needed to discover the hidden face of Afghanistan and enter the interior world, really cross the threshold of the family home, where, as a woman, I would be admitted. I quickly understood that this is where the inner life of the country lay. There I met those on whose shoulders rests the entire social structure, those who are silent in front of men but who play a dominant role in the economy and in family decisions. As a woman and a mother like them, having come from some other place they couldn't imagine for lack of any models, familiar and foreign at the same time, I spoke their language and understood them.

This alchemy was very important, for it helped them talk about themselves openly. My own ignorance about Afghan culture would guide my questions and give rise to detailed answers on points that would seem obvious to any Afghan.

Right from the start, these women seduced me and I loved them. With them I found no trace of the raw contradictions, the blatant honor code, of all the things that create barriers between Afghan men and Europeans. With rare exception, I never felt any obstacle or rift between these women and myself; we were totally compatible. I was bringing them a whiff of air from the outside, and they helped me travel through a foreign land: it was a perfectly balanced exchange.

With the rightness of their gestures and their words, they induced such a fascination in me that I never had to underplay my education and my culture in front of them. They were so authentic that I could at last be myself in Afghanistan.

I didn't have the chance to get to know any Uzbek or Turkoman women, who from early childhood on are fettered to the craft of weaving.

I only spent a little time among the nomads, whose life is even rougher than that of the others, for the life of the men in these conditions is also harsher. But for all of these women, Tajik, Hazara, Pashtun, Uzbek, Turkoman, Pashaï, Nuristani, or Balutsh, the program is laid out from birth: they will be mothers and they will work in order to live.

Afghan women are often oppressed, veiled, cloistered, sometimes muzzled, but it is difficult to speak of these women in terms we would use—the terms of a society in which women have gained enough freedom to be fully aware of their rights, by sometimes furiously opposing the power of man's inertia and complacency that would have gladly left them where they were, namely, in the home. Still, one need not accept the unacceptable for all that.

All I wanted to do was let them speak. May each person learn from and reflect upon this, as I have done.

"If I don't speak to you, when will I again have the opportunity to be heard?"

That is the only reason for this book—to give Afghan women the opportunity to be heard; confidences made to a woman with no male intermediary, which inevitably would have stopped them in their tracks or distorted their words.

On the surface, there is no history of Afghan women, for history seems to have been made without them; they are today as they were thirteen centuries ago.

King Amanullah, who reigned from 1919 to 1929, had encouraged women's emancipation in his grandiose plan to modernize the
country. Men were to abandon traditional dress upon entering Kabul
and put on Western clothing. And during one official ceremony, the
monarch solemnly lifted the veil of his wife, Soraya, in front of all the
kingdom's dignitaries. In 1920, he proclaimed new laws concerning
marriage and repudiation.

"Oh, my most honorable compatriots, obey the order of God! If
you fear that you cannot do justice to many, then one wife will suf-
fice. For having two wives without being just is to be guilty toward
God."

All he was doing was calling to mind sura 4, verse 3 of the Koran.

But the mullahs were frightened, and in a military coup the Tajik
Batcha-e Saqao ("son of the water carrier") seized power, which he
held on to for nine months in 1929. This was time enough to promise the return to Islam and an immediate halt to women's emancipation, which was just barely being born. He declared himself ready
to slay any man whose beard was shaped in Western style and any
woman who wore her hair cut short.

Nader Shah took the throne again from 1929 to 1933 and ordered his wives to wear the veil so as to keep the mullahs pacified.
It was Queen Homaïra, the wife of Zaher Shah (1933–1973), who
would take up the offensive again by creating the first "Institute
of Afghan Women" in 1946. In 1959, she bolstered Prime Minister Mohammad Daoud Khan's initiative aimed at suppressing
the chador, the full-length pleated veil that wraps a woman from
head to toe, leaving just a small, embroidered mesh opening in
front of her face that hardly allows her to see and only barely to
breathe. It was the institute's goal to protect women, mothers,
and children. Obviously it affected an infinitesimal percentage of
Afghan women—some urban women who were mentally ready
to call upon an organization of this kind. The so-called charity
committee was financed by donations from great merchants and

affluent families, received no government aid, and represented the good work of privileged women. Elsewhere was the mass of those who did not go out, not even if veiled. And the chador, which had been the prerogative of middle-class women to abandon, was now adopted by the urban working class.

On the occasion of the Year of the Woman in 1975, the spokesmen for President Mohammad Daoud Khan (1973–1978) announced:

> Marriages will be arranged only with the full consent of
> man and woman; the Afghan woman, like the Afghan man,
> has the right to self-determination; women and men have
> equal rights before the court, without discrimination in the
> penal codes; women have the right to choose their career
> and the kind of education they wish to obtain.

In reality, if they are not already engaged from early childhood on, it is still rare for young people in the rural areas to be consulted, and there boys have hardly any greater freedom than girls in making their choice. In extreme cases, a young man can grab a girl by force; with a rifle shot in the air, he challenges whoever would like to ask for her in marriage; if she is not given to him, she will be married to no one else, for he will declare himself ready to initiate a vendetta.

In middle-class families, should a daughter be consulted before being married off, it is her education that will restrict her parents' choice. Since she has no opportunity to meet any boys, she refuses the first suitor—she is eighteen years old and doesn't know him. Nor does she know the second one, for that matter. Then, with the fourth or fifth suitor, she feels impelled to accept the unknown young man since her parents are beginning to grow irritated and she herself is afraid of ending up an old maid. However, this one may be no better than the first admirer was.

A girl has no right to go out without permission. Her brothers supervise her, and later on, if her husband forbids it, she will not be able to work outside the home.

If a woman asks for a divorce, the man has the right to keep the children, whom he will entrust to his own family, for the mother—like a leper—will presumably contaminate them. He also has the right to keep everything in the house.

Little rural girls rarely go to school and then are removed as soon as they reach puberty.

When the Communists took power in 1978, they put a woman named Anahita Ratebzada in charge; she had been militant from the beginning. If she intended to help women, it was within the framework of the Afghan social revolution, an action that could only be consigned to failure in an unwinnable war against tradition.

Since the fall of the Communists in 1992, the status of women in Afghan society has been in a permanent state of regression. Despite pressure from his allies, Ahmad Shah Massoud, the leader, had kept the posts of television anchorwomen and all civil servants open for them. The education of girls in the schools of the territories he controlled seemed very important to him.

The Taliban wiped the slate clean from the moment they entered the cities, declaring that careers for women were illegal and forcing civil servants, teachers, and all other women working outside the house to withdraw inside their homes. Even little girls were prohibited from being educated. These men have always lived among themselves and know nothing about family life and Afghan customs. Little orphan boys, living in refugee camps, they were the perfect prey for the fanatics who could easily recruit them for military operations.

Historians will certainly be able to shed light on the precise role of bin Laden and his Arab supporters in subjugating the Afghan population to regulations that were totally foreign to the country's culture.

Having grown strong through the many vagaries that have

overturned their lives for more than twenty years now, will women's voices finally be heard?

In the history of their own country, they have always played a fundamental role. Their stories show this clearly: they are mistresses in their own homes, and many a man is merely the spokesman for his own spouse on the outside.

 # Marriage

The life of an Afghan woman revolves around one major event—marriage. She is prepared for it and often merely submits to it, later giving it meaning through motherhood.

In Afghanistan, boys and girls who grow up in the same house live in two different worlds from childhood on. The little boy is being prepared for his social role: his father initiates him into the mechanisms of the world of men and its passions—horses, battles of all kinds, a thousand and one athletic distractions, and, above all, its code of honor, which is of particular importance in Pashtun society. The young man quickly knows himself to be adult through his relationship with the women for whom he is responsible, a mother and sisters to whose virtue his honor is tied.

The Koran states that sons and daughters are gifts from God, and yet gunshots are fired only to greet the birth of a future warrior. Parents are rarely thrilled at the arrival of a daughter, for she is born to enrich another home while a son will remain with his father, bolstering the heritage he will have to protect. And then, as everywhere else in the world, if a daughter leads a loose life she brings shame to the family much more readily than a son who shows no respect for the customs.

The little girl grows used to her family role, for she is born to become a mother and lives life in a rhythm of acquiescence to men. Household tasks become second nature to her. It is still quite normal to see her at age five or six taking care of the baby, whom she carries around on her hip like a grown woman.

The Afghan home is not a diminished cell—while the father is alive, brothers live together around the same courtyard with their wives and children. If, from puberty onward, a young girl must hide her face from strangers, leave school where she has just barely learned to read and write—in short, avoid showing herself outside the house—she does not, however, live in a cloister. She is free to see her male cousins and have a good time with them, as long as she is not betrothed to one of them, for in that case any association would be judged immodest and she would have to avoid him until the day of her wedding.

Traditionally, there are many marriages between blood relations in Afghanistan. They say that these unions are heaven-blessed. The land, which is sacred, will remain in the family at the time of inheritance; the stronger the family, the better one's life. Sometimes the survival of the group actually depends on these same-family unions.

On the other hand, many marriages are made between families who are friends or otherwise associated—someone has a newborn baby daughter whom he promises to his best friend for his son. The dowry is to be paid by the boy's family, and sometimes the first daughter-in-law has "cost" so much that the father-in-law no longer has much left to give for marrying his second son; he then gives one of his daughters to the family of this son's fiancée in exchange. Another kind of event can also occur. In the countryside, the daughter of Mohamed Khan had taken off with a boy from a neighboring tribe. To prevent a vendetta, Mohamed Khan was forced to accept a daughter of the other family for one of his sons as compensation— like an exchange of cattle.

In many cases in Kabul young people choose each other according to a codified ritual.

On a street corner, Sultân, who is some twenty years old, caught the quickly averted glance of a young high school girl who was on her way to buy bread. The next day, at the same time and in the same place, he sees her again and so it goes for several days; but now she is haughty and inaccessible. He is in love, as is she; but not a word, not a look may betray her. Sultân does not speak to her: this would be impolite. He sends his mother and sisters on the trail; they will be his matchmakers. They are going to enter into an in-depth investigation of the young woman—her age, her qualities, the social status of her parents, the family's practices, for they want to avoid having a Sunni (orthodox) marry a Shiite (renegade), nor should he marry beneath him.

The house and the girl are quickly found. Sultân's messengers—his mother, one aunt, and an older sister—have the mission of extracting the exquisite bird.

They knock on the door, and the simpler the pretext the better: "It is hot, may God be with you. Would you perhaps have a glass of water for us?" In Kabul, a mother is not easily fooled when she has a daughter to be married off.

They sit down and the conversation stays superficial: "What a lovely house you have . . . ," until the moment when a young girl comes in with the tea tray. Sultân's sister is briefly surprised: she doesn't recognize the chosen one her brother had discreetly pointed out to her in the street. The hostess hastens to introduce the young girl as her oldest daughter, already engaged. The emissaries relax with a sigh of relief, for if she were still to be married off, there would be no question of showing an interest in the younger one. The rumor would start that the oldest one has a defect to hide.

The women have been watching each other; they get along and make a plan to see each other again when Nasrîn, the favored one, is to be introduced to them.

In the country, future mothers-in-law sometimes put the young girl through a complete test: she has to walk with a jug on her head to show she doesn't limp; she has to thread a needle to prove that her eyesight is good; she is asked whether she can cook, embroider, and if she is prepared to work from morning to night.

In Kabul, Sultân has made his choice and it is no longer his mother's role to continue the discussion. Fortunately, the father has agreed. This time, the women's delegation is going to make the official proposal.

Nasrîn has made a lightning appearance to welcome them. It wouldn't be right for her to be present at the conversation. She is pretty, although not in line with the canons of classical beauty, which are a slender bust, broad hips, heavy thighs, small feet, light skin, pink cheeks, a sweet face as round as the moon, small mouth, elegant fine nose, large black eyes, and thick hair the color of the night crowning her face.

"By the grace of God, you have a very beautiful daughter. My husband sings the praises of your home and speaks of the honor it will bring him to unite our two families. My son, Sultân, may God be praised, is well bred and has all the qualities for making a good husband. If you accept, I am certain that he will always prove himself to be humble and obedient to you and that he will make your daughter happy."

Nasrîn's mother says very little. With lowered eyes, she listens and at the end graciously expresses her gratitude. She adds that they are doing them a great honor but that her daughter is quite young, barely fifteen years old; that, even if she performs all domestic tasks well, she doesn't yet know anything about life's difficulties. She will speak to her husband about it. The women go home.

A certain interlude will go by during which the parents of the girl, too, will make their inquiries. Sultân's family continues to send courteous messages at regular intervals. The wait increases the girl's value. If she were to be given away too quickly, it would be a sign of their being in a hurry to get rid of her and therefore that she is "worth" nothing. They say that the young man's parents should wear their shoes out until the soles have become "as thin as garlic skins"!

Sometimes the daughter is consulted, but more often than not she is not included in the discussions. Her behavior is codified: if she smiles or weeps soundlessly, she accepts; if she sobs and cries, she does not agree. Generally, there is no scandal since boys and girls are not in the habit of discussing a father's decisions.

Now the men take the business in hand. They are going to decide on the *tuyana,* the marriage price. The future husband must pay his father-in-law a sum of money that can vary greatly depending on circumstances and ethnicity.

This custom, which has been abandoned by the Kabul middle class, remains very much alive everywhere else, even though King Amir Abdul Rahman officially prohibited its practice at the end of the nineteenth century. To enhance his prestige, the bridegroom must do things generously, and if he is not rich he has to borrow money from loan sharks, sometimes putting himself in debt for life. They even say that among the Turkomans in the north of the country, where girls weave carpets from a very young age on and are an important source of income for the household, it was the custom to kidnap the chosen girl in order to force the father to accept a reparation for the offense and be separated from his precious daughter by accepting a sum that would be more than a hundred thousand afghani (in 1978, the average monthly salary was a thousand afghani).

The sums of money, paid with the official goal of compensating a father for his daughter's departure, represent anywhere from a few months' to a few years' salary or else a part of the family capital in heads of cattle. For this reason, many boys cannot dream of getting married before they have reached a certain age and have enough savings to afford it. This poses quite a few problems in a society where relations between the two sexes are prohibited outside of marriage.

The fiancé is also the one who makes a gift of a complete trousseau for the young girl and takes care of the expenses of the wedding celebration. The trousseau and jewelry will continue to be the bride's property.

The day of the engagement has been set. Everyone is excited. For the women it will be an opportunity to meet their female friends and relatives, to dance and sing. It is the day of *shirîni-khorî*, "of eating sweets." Nasrîn's mother has invited close relatives, at most some twenty people. She has prepared a whole series of teapots and mounds of cookies. Sultân's family arrives. In the countryside, this would be a procession accompanied by the sound of drums or gunshots fired by young men. The family brings many presents, stacked up on a tray: clothes for the bride-to-be, a white turban for the father, fabric of fine quality for the mother, sweets, and finally—the star of the lot—the *qand*, a sugar bread around which the promise of marriage is to be sealed.

The celebration is in full swing. The old women, sitting to the side, carefully observe the two newly united families and are already spinning many other marriage plans.

Then comes the solemn moment when the *qand* must be broken, which symbolizes the future husband's surrender to his family-in-law. The grandfather breaks off the peak, then everyone in turn takes a piece. "*Mobârak!* Congratulations!" they all cry. They wish each other well. The children share the crumbs. The engagement is official. In keeping with the rules of modesty, Nasrîn has remained in her room, but she knows that from here on in, and in the eyes of the world, she now belongs to Sultân.

The next day, sugared almonds are handed out in the neighborhood to announce the young girl's engagement.

Two years have passed since that day: there has been a death in Sultân's family and then he had to do his military service. The engaged couple will not see each other again before the evening of the wedding.

The young girl is preparing for her future life by being more diligent by her mother's side in the kitchen and with her embroidery work that her sisters-in-law will admire. She thinks ruefully of the one whom she glimpsed one day on the corner of a street. He had fire in his eyes, but is he the Prince Charming of her dreams?

Finally it is time to set the wedding date, and Sultân's parents arrive to discuss the contract. They have collected the embroidered cloths and shawls, the earrings, the heavy bracelets, and the pieces of silver they will give the bride.

About ten women of both families go to the bazaar to buy Nasrîn's clothes, choosing from the finest, that is to say, from the most expensive, materials; fabrics with huge multicolored flowers that each one of them caresses delightedly with the tips of her fingers. Tunics and loose pants will be made of these in which to dress the young woman. A green outfit must be made also for the religious ceremony, the *nékâ,* and a white one for the wedding itself.

It is again the bridegroom's father who must purchase eighty kilos of rice, twenty-eight kilos of fat, fifty kilos of meat, sixty-six kilos of sugared almonds, seven of sugar, green and black tea, flour for the bread, wood for the kitchen stoves, not counting the rental of the enormous pots for the *palaô,* the national rice-based dish. The bus that will take the guests on the ritual tour of the city is also his responsibility.

Invitations are called out: "In the name of Allah, the compassionate and merciful. Sultân, the son of Mohamed Sharîf, will be united with the daughter of Abdul Rassoul . . ."

The marriage is celebrated in the home of the young girl, and the festivities will last for a week, for the guests sometimes arrive two or three days ahead of time, traveling long distances. The celebrations take place on Thursday, Friday—the day of worship—and Saturday.

Wednesday morning Nasrîn is taken to the hairdresser, who curls her hair. Thursday, accompanied by her mother, sister, and mother-in-law, she goes to the *hammam,* the baths, where they will first remove the unwanted hair on her body, which is to be perfectly smooth. Then one of the women washes her feet, another her back; they pour milk over her body; they massage her with sweet almond oil. A cousin has arrived with a tambourine and another sings softly; throughout the process they banter.

Thursday evening (*shaô e khinâ,* or the evening of henna), Nasrîn and Sultân have their hands painted with henna. Everyone around them will have the same thing done, for the henna of a bridal pair brings bliss.

Friday the guests continue to arrive at the house. In the country, this would consist of processions of men, dancing and singing along the way.

They are settling in. Inside, the women are chatting and singing, beating the tambourines. The green clothing has been brought to Nasrîn; the color of Islam is also the color of happiness. They have helped her get dressed. Seated in the back of the room reserved for women, solitary, huddled in her shawl and made up in white to make her more beautiful, she looks like a mask of total indifference—she must not betray her feelings under any circumstances. Joy would hurt her mother, and sadness would be an insult to her mother-in-law.

The men laugh and dance outside, where carpets and cushions have been laid out. Actors are putting on a farcical show. A dancer, made up and dressed like a woman, has come to entertain the guests.

Young boys bring basins in so that everyone can wash the right hand, the hand used to put food in one's mouth. Dishes of *palaô* make the rounds, and people do their best to take the biggest handful of rice. But they are careful to serve the choicest piece of roast lamb to their neighbor. Everyone feasts on crepes stuffed with spinach and on fried eggplant in a creamy sauce made with sheep cheese.

In the afternoon, a small group of men from each of the two families goes to the mosque. A relative represents the bride, who thus will not need to move. Often it is the same for the bridegroom.

The contract and the marriage act will be drawn up before the mullah. The latter reads a few verses of the Koran. Then the question of the *mahr* is brought up, the guarantee granted the young woman by Koranic law that if her husband should want to repudiate her and send her back to her parents, he will have to pay her a sum of money.

On the other hand, if the woman asks for divorce, she will have no right to anything and will run the risk of losing custody over her children.

In the main room at the house, the women have placed a large cushion covered with a white sheet on a kind of a platform. That is where the bride will sit enthroned throughout the celebration.

It is ten o'clock in the evening. Nasrîn is dressed in white and her face is covered with a veil. She will be seeing Sultân for the second time in her life. They enter the room at the same time, and everyone present chants the marriage song, *âhesta boro* ("walk slowly"). They come close together, shoulder to shoulder, without looking at one another. One of them then tries to put a foot on the other one's foot. It is said that the one who succeeds will be the master of the couple. Then they must sit down but at the very same moment, for here, too, should the boy sit down before his wife, then she will dominate him. This gives rise to a whole game between the girls and boys of honor who, standing on either side of the bridal couple, admonish them not to give in. Finally, Nasrîn's father approaches and, putting one hand on each of their shoulders, makes them sit slowly. Everyone applauds.

Then a shawl is spread over the bridal pair; a mirror is given to them in which they are meant to see each other for the first time. This object is a good-luck charm for the woman, who will keep it all her life. The bride's face belongs to the husband; she may not show it to any other man. They are presented with the holy Koran, which they reverently kiss.

Then the *mâlida* is brought to them, a kind of semolina made of crushed fresh bread crumbs, sugar, oil, and spiced with cardamom. Sultân gives some of this in his spoon to Nasrîn, and then she gives some to him.

Everyone present will eat of this after the wedding couple, from the oldest to the youngest.

To amuse the gathering, a herald then reveals the inventory of gifts brought by the guests of both families, punctuating the announcement with little jokes and greeted with applause: "See this now and don't say that they gave nothing to Nasrîn." "Take a good look and don't go saying that Nasrîn's mother was stingy with her son-in-law!" Clothing, shawls, embroidered pillows parade by the eyes of the assembly. "*Nâm e Khodâ!* In the name of God! May their home be blessed!"

The banquet table is festive and rich in color—the platters are overflowing with different kinds of melons, cakes, and *firinî*, creamed rice cakes sprinkled with pistachios, which everyone loves.

By two in the morning, the car for the bridal pair arrives, decorated with many paper flowers. Before she leaves, Nasrîn's father puts a belt around her waist that he tightens until she begins to cry. Then he puts her hand in Sultân's hand: "May God be with you. Take good care of her."

The rest of the group gets into the rented bus to make the ritual tour of the city, the *shahr-gasht*.

All night long, Sultân and Nasrîn will stay awake, but their marriage will not be consummated until Saturday evening.

Sunday morning, Sultân will slip out to go and take the ritual bath at the hammam, since according to Koranic law one should purify oneself after every sexual encounter.

That is when Nasrîn will return the white sheet that her mother without a word of explanation had given her the evening before. Stained with blood, it is the irrefutable proof of the young girl's virginity and the honor of her home. All the women will see it and be able to announce the news.

Now Nasrîn has entered the home of her father-in-law. Someday she will have to ask her mother-in-law for permission to visit her own family. For one month, she will be coddled and looked after, will not touch or drink any cold water, and will avoid any hard work, in case she is to be blessed by God and becomes pregnant.

Motherhood

The value of girls lies first in the hymen and then in male children: if only daughters are born, the inheritance would be broken up at the death of their father, since girls leave the paternal home to join that of their husbands.

The young bride's virginity on the wedding night is the guarantee of undefiled motherhood. If the bride should not be a virgin, she will be sent back immediately to her father and the money spent for the wedding will be reclaimed.

This is what women repeatedly say when they are together, but in reality the occasion almost never presents itself. And if the betrothed pair should have committed an indiscretion before the wedding, a pigeon's blood will be used to stain the sheet.

A Pashtun poem says, "Oh, may my wife be fertile soil and of my sons may there be a hundred!"

A woman from Paghman, a small town just a few kilometers outside of Kabul, recounts that for the first birth all the women in the family were present at the child's arrival. Sometimes there are fifteen or twenty gathered around the pregnant woman.

First they massage her belly so that the baby will be in the right position. Then, when the contractions become stronger, they make her crouch above a basin with her forehead leaning against the tray of the *sandali*.[1]

---

[1] This is a brazier around which the family gathers in winter. It is often minus twenty degrees centigrade in Kabul in the winter.

In the traditional home there is no other furniture besides the
sandali. Normally, people sleep on mattresses on the floor covered
with kilims or carpets that are folded and put away in a corner of the
room during the day.

The child is born into the pan above which the woman has been
crouching. An experienced woman cuts the umbilical cord, leaving
the length of the palm of a hand, and ties it. They say that if it is a
boy it will fall off after six days, eleven if it's a girl. The young mother
is given a solid fortifying tonic of eggs and *lîtî,* a kind of soup made
with flour roasted in oil, to which sugar, water, and raisins are added.
In principle, she will rest for two weeks during which time the child
is never left alone, for evil genies could abduct it. Its fingernails will
not be cut, for then it would have no defense against the quibbling
spirit disturbing its sleep.

In the country people are afraid of the hospital: "That is where
you go to die!" According to Doctor Trina of the Masturat Hospital
in Kabul, Pashtun women are the most difficult to take care of because they refuse to have themselves examined, even by a woman.
If retention of the placenta is the problem, they kill a goat whose
skin is placed on the mother's belly; if there is no delivery within
twenty-four hours, it will be a sheep's skin, and finally that of a cow.
When a young mother, burning with fever, goes to the hospital with
septicemia, she has to climb the steps by herself. Often it is too late,
and she cannot be saved.

Woman as a sexual object counts for nothing; only the mother
is worthy of respect. Consequently, a childless woman has no reason
to exist, for she is not fulfilling her role and could fear being repudiated by her husband, which would leave her impoverished and
without any hope of remarrying.

The disgrace is first of all social. Amina has been married for thirteen years. Her sister-in-law grumbles aggressively: "I've dropped
them so many times, like an animal, and she can't even deliver a

blind one!" The family refuses to understand her husband, who will not take another wife: he loves her.

Laïli is fifteen when she marries. On their wedding night, her very much older husband explains to her that he is impotent and previously has always turned away any chance to get married. But at her father's urging and tormented by the idea that he would have to reveal his humiliating secret, he has given in this time. He asks the young woman to swear she will keep the truth from everyone and never say a word, no matter what happens.

She swears, even though in such cases Koranic law gives her the right to set herself free. For ten years she will play the role he requires of her, going to the hammam as he does to pull the wool over everyone's eyes by making people believe they have had sexual relations, which demand purification. Thus, she is taking the stigma of sterility upon herself and endures the mothers, sisters, or neighbors who incessantly come by for news, pestering her about her belly that won't grow and constantly increasing their reproaches or advice.

Finally, her old husband falls ill and dies.

She is still young and custom requires that a brother or cousin of her husband's marry her, but her in-laws don't want to hear about her anymore. She is arid soil that should not be cultivated, and so she is sent back to her father.

She is twenty-five and luckily she is quite beautiful. One of her first cousins agrees to take her under his wing and marries her. The truth comes out—she was a virgin! The new husband proclaims the news to anyone willing to listen. The in-laws, filled with remorse, send a delegation to the young woman to offer their apologies. Why had she not said anything? They would have recognized her worth.

I have known several cases in which a young woman who was not able to have children was "given" an infant by her sister or sister-in-law so that she might raise it as her own child. This kind of generosity is actually encouraged by the fact that they all live in the same house and that the relationships between large and small are governed more by generational differences than by the personal bonds between individuals.

Latifa's mother has four children. The last one was just a few months old when her husband took another wife. He left to go and live with her in the provinces, abandoning the first wife in Kabul without any resources. Let her manage somehow; he is no longer interested in her. He left the children with her, and she will do everything possible to educate them. They will go to university because that is what she wants. What courage, what deprivations, what sacrifices she must have suffered, and what strength she must have had. What quantities of laundry she must have washed; how many houses she must have scrubbed just to have her four children gather around some bread and soup every day! Every year, she would add a piece of fabric to lengthen the pants of her son who was attending secondary school, where he was doing brilliant work at the same desks as the sons of the royal family. Everything these children are they owe to her woman's hands. A magnificent mother!

Women are mothers above all. Yet, it should not be forgotten that before the war 50 percent of the country's economy rested on their work, both in the cities and on the land.

 Work

In the City

In 1974, in Afghanistan's large cities and depending on social class, there were female physicians, nurses, school teachers, university professors, office employees, merchants in the modern districts (the bazaar being strictly for men), bakers in the noncommercial areas, and factory workers. The former frequently came from affluent families who would live halfway between tradition and modernity. This, however, was not the case for those working for the company where raisins were cleaned in Kabul or for the women bakers.

After the harvest, a portion of the grapes that have been sun-dried is sent to Kabul. The establishment where these are cleaned and sorted employs about two hundred people—one workshop for men and two for women who work every day, including Fridays, the Muslim day of worship. Time off goes unpaid, as do sick days. In 1978, a female employee was earning thirty-three afghani a day; a man would make forty-five. It should be noted that at the time a kilo of meat cost sixty afghani on the average, a pound of tea, eighty afghani, a *sêr* (seven kilos) of rice was one hundred and forty afghani, and a *sêr* of flour, eighty.

Seniority does not count and every female worker receives the same salary. One sees mainly chadors on the coat racks, for it is the women of the working classes who wear the veil fully covering them in the street.

Adela, "the Just," is twenty-three years old. Married at age twelve, she now has four children. Her husband is in the military in Mazar-i-Sharif, the big city in the north. She is his second wife.

"He married me because the other one kept losing every one of her children at birth. Since I am with them, the other woman's children have survived as well; she has only two of them because she is old. Since she was working at the factory I wanted to do the same. My husband was opposed to this because I was still young, but the boss told him that if he didn't want me to work he only had to lock me up when he went out. Thanks to that I can send my son to school. The other wife and I put our money together when we get paid, every two weeks, and we go to the bazaar."

"Are you happy with your life?"

"I am happy with my children."

Zarmina, "Her friendship is golden," is a fourteen-year-old school-girl. After retiring, her father has just enough to feed his children.

"I work on Fridays and during the vacation to help my family and buy my notebooks and books for school."

Zohra (her name is the name of a star): "I have been working here for three years. I went to school until seventh grade. We used to have an easy life then, but my father became ill. He married three times. His first wife died, but the two others are alive, and one of those is my mother. Then there are fifteen children, and my father passed away last month. My other brothers and sisters have given up their studies, too. My sister who is thirteen works here with me; so does my mother, as forewoman. We are very poor."

Mina, "Calyx": "I was very young when I was married to a man who mistreated me. I was locked up in the house. He would go to the bazaar, bring back something to eat but never anything else. I had a four-year-old son and an eighteen-month-old daughter. He repudiated me without returning my dowry to me and took away my children. I remarried a first cousin so that I wouldn't have to live with my brothers. My son comes to see me sometimes, but they must have told my daughter, who is now fifteen, some horror stories about me, because I've never seen her again."

Parwîn (again the name of a star): "I was widowed and, through my employment in this workshop, made friends with a woman who married me off to her brother: she is the one who arranged everything. Since then, my husband left to look for work in Iran because he couldn't find anything here. He writes only to his mother and I never hear a word from him."

Laïli is her husband's second wife. Why did he marry her?

"His first wife had married off their oldest daughter without consulting him. She tricked him and he simply wanted to take revenge, that's all. Of the nine children I gave birth to, only four are alive."

She is pregnant again and asks me how to go about not having children anymore. Like many other women, she has tried the pill but it made her sick. When new mothers come out of the maternity clinic the midwives actually suggest means of contraception, and the pill is available in Kabul's pharmacies.

Bîbîgol, "Lady Flower": "When the man comes home from work, he has nothing else to do. Besides the grapes at the factory, we have the cooking and the housekeeping to do at home; and we take care of the children."

During the day, children are watched by an oldest daughter (from the age of five or six on, a little girl is quite capable of being responsible for the younger ones), a mother-in-law, or a sister-in-law.

Most of the husbands are old men who can no longer work. "But they behave better!" the women say as they burst out laughing.

Usually, bread is baked at home; in principle, every home has a tandour, a bread oven that consists of an earthenware liner placed in a hole in the ground. In the country, women bake one day at this one's house and the next day at a neighbor's house. In the cities, however, families are splintered and women more isolated. Therefore, when they lived in areas far from the bazaar run by men, they began to create women's bake houses.

They prepare the dough at home—"the bread is better because you know what goes into it"—and then they bring this in huge cloth-covered bowls to the bakery.

This is a tiny room in the center of which the tandour is burning brightly. The two women who do the baking are crouched on the ground, their heads wrapped in a piece of fabric, their eyes burning from the heat. The first one puts her arm in the white-hot stove to press the flat round loaves against the earthenware walls, after having first moistened her hand wrapped in a piece of cloth. The customers have lined up their balls of dough on a wooden plank next to her. Her colleague takes the golden bread out with a scraper and a long-handled hook.

The bakers' day begins before sunrise in order to light the stove, which they will keep feeding with wood until the evening hours.

At the bakeries in the bazaar one bread costs two afghanis. The earnings of these women cannot be calculated on the same basis, since the clients themselves supply the dough. Based on the rent they pay and the 560 kilos of wood they have to buy each week, they ask half an afghani per loaf. They must bake about eighteen hundred loaves a week to break even. Why all this work? Each customer brings a bowl of flour, a small quantity of which serves to dust the plank on which the balls of dough are placed; the rest is in payment for the bakers' work, as well as for bread for them and their children: minuscule earnings without which they could not survive.

To become a baker poverty really has to have pushed you into a corner. In fact, these women have turned to the only profitable activity they feel capable of taking up: baking bread the way their mothers, grandmothers, and great-grandmothers did.

The life of the Afghan people, like that of the greater majority of the Third World's population, rests on a very fragile balance. The war has brought about catastrophe in these societies that were quietly pursuing their path toward modernity. For those of us living in wealthy, democratic nations, holidays, vacation, savings, and travel have meaning and are important everyday concerns. We often forget that these are privileges the vast majority of human beings cannot even imagine.

In the Country

Nuristan, the mountainous province southeast of Kabul, converted to Islam and was belatedly attached to the rest of Afghanistan in 1896; it became the first province in the country to rebel against the Communist government in 1978.

I met Begom in 1977, during a hike in upper Nuristan, where trucks and cars cannot go. The rules of civility demand that a traveler can stay, for three days at the very most, with someone offering hospitality. This was an extraordinary opportunity as it allowed me to follow the young Nuristan woman from morning to evening, step by step through her daily life. I have a photo of her against the light at the door of the mill. She and her baby are smiling at me. It is one of those moments of pure bliss when harmony reigns and you forget time and space.

Shoukour, her husband, came to visit us one day in Kabul with some of his brothers. As a gift he brought us the skin of a bear he had killed.

In the villages of Nuristan, the women seem freer than in the rest of the country. They do not cover their faces when a stranger approaches. But, in contrast to the boys and men, they do not linger to watch travelers—they don't have a minute to spare.

Before the conquest by Islam, this region was known as Kafiristan, "the land of pagans"; Nuristan means "land of light." In his book *The Kafirs of the Hindu-Kush,* George S. Robertson, an English traveler, described these women as they were in 1896. They carried enormous baskets on their back, sometimes filled with stones to build their houses, sometimes with bunches of grapes to make wine or with wheat to be pounded. They are harnessed to the most onerous tasks, slaves of the home, makers of babies, and workers in the fields.

Begom is their sister.

She is fifteen. Tajik and thus Persian-speaking, she is originally from Badakhshan, where they say the prettiest girls of Afghanistan come from.

She was not yet born when her father crossed the mountain passes into Nuristan. That is where she grew up and was married off. She is Shoukour's second wife; he is around forty, as is his first wife. But while he has stayed young and can gallop in the mountains chasing ibex and bear, she, the "older one," is an old woman with a bad back, eyes burned by smoke, and hands that are cracked from the icy water of the rivers. Three years ago, Shoukour took Begom because the older one could no longer do anything and a twelve-year-old is already accustomed to the tasks that await her. She has been going to the fields with her mother since she learned to walk; her eyes have grown used to the smoky atmosphere of the house, whose only ventilation comes through the door; her back is well acquainted with the heavy baskets of wood gathered in the forest or full of the soil with which to build and fortify irrigation canals. At the age of twelve, Begom was not surprised to be married to a man who is older than her father, for nothing is more normal. And besides, in the village Shoukour has the reputation of being a very good man. He is handsome, with black hair that he wears long, a ring in his ear, and light blue eyes he accentuates with kohl. Respectful of the convention, the man waited for the young woman to have her first period before touching her. At fourteen, Begom has a son, a true little doll.

Ask a Nuristan man to tell you about the division of labor in the family. He will answer you very simply that the women do everything. And what about the men? Oh, basically nothing!

In the summer, Shoukour and his family live in Naghar, up in the mountains high above the valley beyond Barg e Matal, the last town of the Kamdesh Valley that trucks can reach. Their winter village is called Peshawurak.

Begom gets up before dawn to go and collect wood. She comes back home and starts the fire, inside, right on the ground. There is no window and the door is the only opening onto the outside. The house is small: one room for the family, one for guests.

Begom kneads the dough for bread; wheat flour for special occasions but corn for the daily bread. The iron plate above the fire is hot; on this she bakes round loaves and flat ones like pancakes. The baby cries, she puts him to her breast. She prepares Shoukour's breakfast with warm milk, fat, and bread. They throw a pot of water on the fire. It is time to go out.

The man is going to check on the herd and milk the cow and goats with his other son.

Begom quickly cleans up the baby, wraps him up, and puts him back to bed. She has to make the rounds of her three or four terraced fields. To set them up she had to cart many huge baskets of soil. It was she, too, who smoked the earth before the first snowfalls and who worked the soil. She dug the irrigation canals, seeded, hoed, and nurtured the wheat she now tenderly caresses. She gets up several times a night to redirect the channels, let the water run from one field to another and to skillfully adjust the flow. If he doesn't have any business in the village, Shoukour will help her with the harvest.

There is no more flour in the house, and grain will have to be taken down to the mill, at the foot of the mountain on the banks of the river. She reaches into the reserve, a small stone structure that serves as a granary, then spreads the grain out on a surface she has carefully swept clean and winnows it together with the first wife, as they talk.

They are lucky enough to get along well; the older one treats the little one as if she were her daughter, and they are very fond of each other. Begom feels sorry for the woman who has given their husband so many children and worn herself out doing the tasks she herself is all too familiar with. She doesn't resent doing the laundry while the other wife is nuzzling the baby in her lap. The older woman had been invaluable to the younger one during the delivery, isolated as she was in the middle of the mountains, far from the traditional village midwife. Furthermore, everything had gone very smoothly—Begom was so young.

The grain is clean. She fills her huge basket and goes down the path leading to the mill. It is deserted and she'll come back later when the miller is there to start the heavy millstone. Going back up, she stops in at her sister's. That poor woman is not as lucky as Shoukour's wives: her husband, who is young and always in a jealous rage, prevents her from speaking to anyone at all and beats her on the slightest pretext.

Begom hears Shoukour calling her. He has brought in the milk, which he is churning on his knees in a goatskin whose openings, legs and neck, he has tied with braided goat hair. He takes the butter out, lets it drain, and then puts it in a plate filled with water. Begom lights the fire under a pot and lets the milk curdle in it to make the cheese she will then put down in tightly squeezed little balls. Her husband will enjoy grilling them at the end of a stick for his lunch.

While her son is nibbling on a piece of bread at her feet, she washes the bits of fabric in which she wraps him and one of the first wife's two dresses in whey. According to her, this liquid, left over from making the butter, is better than soap, and, since there is still some left, she washes her hair as well.

Shoukour watches her tenderly; she is so sweet, the younger one. She braids her long black hair again and quickly puts on her veil, embarrassed to be bareheaded. Then she hangs the laundry on the branches of a nearby shrub and sits down next to her husband, who is playing with the child; the little one jumping from one arm to the other and squealing with laughter.

The older woman brings out some fabric with bright-colored flowers that the husband bought in the city. They can make new cushions for the guestroom and are happily measuring the new yardage.

Evening falls. More bread has to be baked. When she lays out the last pancake on the rounded plate, Begom's eyes are stinging. She admits to a persistent headache. She is in a hurry to go to bed after first feeding and changing the baby.

But outside the hooves of a horse are heard; one of her brothers-in-law is coming to visit, tired after a long day's travel. He will be Shoukour's guest for the night. He is already chasing after a chicken whose throat he slits against the corner of a wall. The pot with water is ready for the plucking. Begom prepares the bird and, besides making the daily soup of fat and cheese, she bakes rolls stuffed with cheese in honor of the guest. The men are talking in the other room, very comfortable on the new cushions. It is deep in the night when the young woman goes to bed, her little one held close. In another hour or two, she will get up again to irrigate her fields.

In this particular home, the man is good and intelligent. He has never beaten his wives, jokes with the "kid," and continues to be affectionate with the older one. His role is a social one. He brings back trophies from the hunt, which is more a pleasure than a means of feeding the family. He knows all the Nuristani games: shooting the stone bow, throwing pebbles, sprint races. He often spends the rest of his time sitting in front of the house of this or that friend, busy chatting and gossiping about whose secret only the men know.

At fifteen, Begom is still very pretty. Robertson observed that in Kafiristan the men were often quite handsome, but the women, because of the work they had to do and the constant exposure to a harsh climate, were rarely attractive. "It is surprising," he added, "to see to what extent some of the young girls already seem old."

Begom silently watches her co-wife, the old woman she will be tomorrow.

The memory is intact but as if frozen in time, and I have trouble imagining Begom twenty-three years later, her son twenty-four years old, older than my own, who at that time had not yet been born. I know she certainly has had other children, and I am trying to forget that in rural Afghanistan, even in times of peace, infant mortality is high. When one would ask a mother how many children she had, she would always mention the living children but not without stating that she had given birth to twice as many but that God had taken them back again.

Nuristani culture is unusual, but all rural Afghan women had one point in common: they did not wear the chador, which every woman today is obliged to wear in the cities. In different colors and styles depending on region and ethnicity, the veil in the country would not cover up their face, and women considered it adequate to turn their heads when passing someone unknown to them.

From Mother to Daughter

The Hazara are originally an ancient group that acquired a Mongolian strain. Sedentary people living on the high central plateau, quite a large number of them settled in the city where, driven by poverty, they accepted the most miserable jobs. Some of them, thanks to their hard work and intelligence, ended up well placed in commerce or education. They have often been spurned by the other ethnic groups because, in a country where the majority is Sunni, they opted for Shiism like their Iranian neighbors.

In the countryside, whether they be Persian-speaking Tajik, Nuristani, Pashtun, or Hazara, inhabitants of the mountains, valleys, or the high plateaus, women lead almost the same existence.

Before Nour Khânom and Laïli describe their life, it is important to situate Hazarajad, "land of the Hazara," at two specific points in its history.

Hazarajad 1971–1972: "In 1970 and 1971, it almost did not snow," writes Mike Barry in *Afghanistan* (Seuil, 1974), citing the agony of a starving region. "International aid sends grain that doesn't reach the people but fills the granaries of the provincial governors and of the corrupt Arbâbs, who are in charge of distributing the wheat to the peasants."

Hazarajad 1980: Famine once again threatens central Afghanistan. The agrarian reform not only never took place, it also completely disrupted the way in which farms had been run. In 1979, families were forced to eat the grain that was meant to be the seed for the following season. They have nothing left.

In 1999, 2000, and 2001, famine and drought caused the exodus of some 25 percent of the population.

The Taliban government completed the ruination of the country.

In 1977, Laïli was working for us and taking care of the children. She was a lively little woman who had the gift of gab. She was about thirty years old and already had seven children. We used to talk a good deal, and she always surprised me with her excellent judgment and humor, which she demonstrated at every turn. It was with her that I decided to embark upon the systematic enterprise of recording Afghan women's accounts, as I have explained. The idea pleased her right away and she had me meet her mother, who told me the story of her life, making an effort to go back to her earliest memories.

They are Ismaelian Shiites. Their story begins in Hazarajad early in the 1920s and continues in Kabul in the poor areas on the edge of the city. When they speak of the house, this often is really nothing but a single room of clay and straw whose floor of trodden earth is covered with woven mats or kilims. The furniture consists of mattresses and blankets, kitchen utensils, and the *sandali* in the winter. Personal effects are contained in a few bundles. There is rarely any running water, which is found in the courtyard at best.

The Story of Nour Khânom, Lady-Light

I was three months old when my mother died. My father quickly remarried. When I was seven, I was taking the cows and sheep to pasture in the mountain close to Turkman, the village where I was born, near Behsud in Hazara country.

When I came back home, my stepmother would vent all her anger on me and give me nothing to eat. A neighbor used to feed me on the sly; she'd put a few biscuits in my belt and I'd leave again for two or three days, with an empty stomach.

My stepmother was never kind to me in any way. If someone was telling stories, during the hottest time of the day, people would be sitting in the shade around that person. She would say to me: "Get up! This is none of your business, go do your work!" She'd keep me away from reunions, celebrations, and marriages. My place was elsewhere: "Go take the animals away, clean the stable and the house!" I didn't know how to sew or embroider.

Once back from the mountain, I'd take care of her children; like a servant, I'd sweep the courtyard, prepare the tandour— I was too little to bake bread. If she made a mistake or did something foolish, she'd take revenge on me and beat me.

One day she had beaten me so badly that I had a hole in my skull. When my father came home he asked me: "What happened, little girl?" Because I was afraid, I told him that a stone had fallen on my head and made the hole while I was climbing the mountain. My father liked me well enough, but he didn't realize how cruel his wife was. My mother—for that is what you also call your stepmother—burned a piece of cloth and put it on my wound, wrapping my head. Nobody touched it again for a month. I was disgusting, full of lice. My maternal grandmother had me come to her to clean me up. Weeping, she kept repeating: "Your mother is dead, why are you alive? If only you had a mother to wash you! You are burdened with all the worries of the house, and she doesn't lift her little pinkie to take care of you!"

She had a meal prepared for me and I ate my fill. But when I came back, my stepmother was furious: "Where were you? Do we starve you so you can go begging elsewhere?"

I cried and said that my grandmother had scrubbed my head. As she beat me, she kept saying that she would kill me if I went back there again: "To hell with you, clean your own filth!"

When would I have had time to do so?

This life went on until I was fourteen. A suitor arrived. My father gave me to him. Yet, he was a handsome man and I was an ugly and dutiful little kid. He hadn't seen me, for our fathers made the arrangements between them: they were friends and happy to tighten their bond with a marriage.

The son said, "I don't love her!" "You'll take her anyway," the father responded. "Whether you love her or not is beside the point! I made the agreement. I didn't choose a girl off the streets for you to have your friends enjoy her, but a woman for your home. She's not the kind who's going to wander around all day long without doing anything. She's a girl, poor thing, who wears herself out working twenty-four hours a day in that house, where she does everything!"

They argued for a long time, but the son couldn't do anything about it.

When he came every other month, he'd lay his head next to the girl of the woods that I was, dirty and emaciated. And I'd cry bitter tears, frightened by the future: I didn't know how to do anything in the house, not even cook a decent meal, nothing of what is usually taught to a daughter. Two years went by.

At the time of our wedding, I had almost no hair: it was always dirty and tangled; nobody had ever cut it or braided it. The mother of my husband took me home with her to get me ready. First she really scrubbed my head and then, hair by hair, removed the lice eggs. I could hear her moan above me: "What have I run into! He went and found me a 'piece of shit' for my son!"

She accused her husband: "This isn't a human being you brought back, this is an animal; no, her face isn't really human!"

I was weeping silently, more and more terrified.

So she cleaned my head and washed me completely. Then

she took very fine black thread and, attaching it to each hair, she made me a hairdo that came down to my waist, so that no one would be able to say her son's fiancée was bald.

My father's wife did nothing for me, didn't even give me a bit of fabric. "Good riddance!" she said.

The wedding took place in Behsud. My husband took me along, just another object among the rest of his things.

As for every young bride, it took me a long time before I could see my father's house again, before the *paï-wâzi*, the first official outing after one is married.

Then my husband settled in Kabul, and as soon as his father died in the village, he had his mother and sisters come to live with us. He didn't hide his loathing for me and would sullenly and ostentatiously turn his back on me at night when going to bed. I was pregnant and that was enough. His mother hated me and began to find girls for him, just to hurt me, who was an idiotic animal, she said, who didn't know how to speak and was ugly to boot. It's true, I was very serious and not at all given to being coy; every little pleasantry, lover's pique, and affectation was foreign to me. I simply wasn't accustomed to that with the life I had led in my father's house.

The following year I had my first son, but he died when he was thirteen days old. He had turned completely purple. Then I began to work in the house of "Hindus," full time. In the evening, I would find my husband as displeased as ever to see me. I cried and said to myself: "Wretch, first I lost my mother, then I was mistreated by my stepmother, and here I am in the house of a husband who hates me as well."

After a year, I began to feel a little better: I used to talk with the woman for whom I worked and who was very good to me. That was a step forward already compared to my life in the country. Then my second son was born.

He was a week old when I had to leave him at home so that

I could go back to work. At six in the morning I would give him milk and come back around seven at night to feed him again. My mother-in-law watched him during the day, but I hadn't been able to find a wet nurse in the family and, besides, we didn't have enough money. We really were just too poor!

I realized that my baby was losing weight. His skin was badly irritated because my mother-in-law didn't change him at all during the day. At seven months, he looked two months old. And I couldn't take him with me for fear I'd lose my job. Thank God, when he was one, my father came to get me to spend some time in Hazarajad with them, for the official visit after a birth. My husband stayed in Kabul, and I left with my son.

I was now a woman, I had a child; smarter than before, I had matured in the capital city. I went from one visit to another. My son began to gain a little weight by eating sheep's cheese and drinking cow's milk: it was a nice year! My husband's mother came to get me back. My father's second wife gave my son a sheep and six *kalema-dâr*,[1] and then we were gone.

Life was hardly livable in Kabul. My husband was very poor; at the time he was selling burning alcohol, which didn't bring in much. His mother and sisters did nothing. I had to work to feed them all, while they were wandering around, eating and sleeping at my expense. When my son turned two, I was expecting the next one and we went back to Hazarajad, hoping to find a better life than in the city: two or three families helping each other in order to draw some food from a plot of land difficult to cultivate.[2]

---

[1] Good luck charms with inscriptions from the Koran.

[2] Polygamy and the wish to have many sons rather than daughters come from the same reasoning: there are more hands to make nature give up what she only surrenders with great difficulty, and therefore better chances for subsistence.

I worked like a man, harder even.

At three in the morning, I would go and gather wood with my husband until sunrise. I would come back to bake bread. Then I'd take the animals out and milk them; I churned the milk to make butter. I cleaned the house. Then I'd go and collect greens in the fields. Not a moment's rest all day long. I would come home exhausted only to find my son sitting in his pee. I'd clean him, change his diaper, and nurse him; he'd calm down. My mother-in-law and her daughters always found something nasty to say to torture me. One might have lost a ring and then accuse me in front of my husband of having stolen it. The other would hide her thimble and needles and blame me for taking them. These were the only times in our life together that my husband beat me: I had dared to complain. Why else would he have done this? Do you beat a table? There were never many arguments between us, but never a kind word either, a nice story, a conversation, a joke, never . . .

The others wanted to instigate a divorce so that he'd bring home a new wife whom they could be proud of. But in the final analysis, I had too many children they would have to take care of if they threw me out.

After three sons, of whom the first one died, I had two little girls.

It was winter, and a lot of snow had fallen. I was busy beating my laundry by the river. An avalanche came down. That evening, when they saw I wasn't coming home, the others began to panic. They came running to the river, where all they found was a pile of snow. Help arrived and all the men in the village began to dig with their spades. After an hour and a half of working, they found my shoes and managed to pull me out very gently. They blew into my ears; I was filled with icy water and shivering beneath the blankets. I could hear them calling me: "Nour Khânom, *yanga, yanga*![3] God be praised, you are alive!"

But no sound would come out of my mouth.

The next day, I was a little better. My seven-month-old daughter was next to me and crying, I put her to the breast. But bad luck for me, during those two days my milk had gone bad and she got sick. She was blind for three months. They had a mullah come who gave her a *tawîz:*[4] he read a few verses from the Koran, wrote them down on a piece of paper that she wore around her neck.

She lasted for a week and then suddenly died. A few days later, my older daughter, who was three and a half, died also; from sadness no doubt: since my accident she was always hanging on to my skirts, no light in her eyes.

You almost never know why a child dies . . .

I'd lost one son, two were alive, and then there were these two daughters who had just died.

We came back to Kabul. Two years later, I was pregnant with my sixth child. We wanted a daughter. I was working hard all day long as a maid, and the house we were renting sat on the side of a hill. Despite my big belly, I would bring up water twice a day from the bottom of the path. I would prepare the bread dough and go back down to have it baked at the bakery.

That is where my first contractions came. I was used to suffering, but all of a sudden there was a terrible pain: "Oh, auntie,[5] quickly bake my bread!"

The woman told me to lie down while she finished her baking. Finally, I went back up to the house, running, with the batch of bread on my head. My mother-in-law, who lived on

---

[3] "Sister-in-law, sister-in-law!"

[4] An amulet.

[5] The baker, who is older, is called "aunt" by her customers. It is also normal to call an older man "uncle." This is a sign of familiarity but also of respect.

the ground floor, had seen me clamber up the stairs four steps at a time to the *kenânârab.*[6] While I was crouching there with a terrible urge, she screamed at me: "May God's fury come down on you, what are you doing delivering a baby there? Get away from that hole!" Then I squatted down above the earth, and she was patting me on the back to help me: two pushes and out it came, like a little cake!

It was a mass of flesh: nothing recognizable, no feet, no hands; the face was just one big swelling: three blobs instead of the eyes and mouth; no nose at all! When I saw that, I thought I'd given birth to a dog; I screamed and fainted. My mother-in-law ripped off a piece of curtain and cleaned everything up, revealing a little girl who had made such an enormous effort to be born that she had become swollen on every side. Everything was twisted, her hands and feet turned backward. When the placenta came out, she called me to wake me up: "Oh, Nour Khânom! Come back to your senses, God is good, you had a daughter! It is a human being. Two of your daughters have gone away, and now you have a new one!"

She carried me on her back because she was tall and strong. She sent one of her daughters to heat up some fat and have me swallow it so I would regain consciousness. But I had been so frightened that I couldn't eat a thing for three days. I opened my eyes to check each one of the baby's limbs.

Ah, if only it hadn't been a girl! A boy, even if deformed, would find a reason to live, but a girl!

Fortunately, there was a *dâî*[7] who lived around the same

---

[6]The toilets.

[7]The *dâî* is the traditional midwife. Often an old woman, she is a healer as well, who knows the traditional remedies that come from plants she finds in the mountain and with which she prepares a variety of brews, herbal teas, unguents or poultices.

courtyard as we, who was the wife of a mullah. She came to re-
assure me: "Don't be so upset, I'm going to straighten out that
little daughter of yours and make her into a human being for you."

She prepared bits of wood and gently adjusted each limb
with bandages, wrapped very, very tightly. Forty days later, when
the bandages were removed, the "something" had become someone. Finally I could feel happy to have a live daughter. Since the
other two had died, I needed to cast a spell on bad fortune.

I never let her wear any new clothes until she was three or
four; I never put any bracelets on her, because her sisters had
worn them. But when she was a little bigger, I played with her as
if she were a doll: I'd braid her hair in fine, tight braids like the
Pashtun nomads, and I'd put pretty clothes on her. My husband,
too, adored her, this little daughter whom we had named Laïli.

After her, I had another boy, marvelous and bright. When
he was just two he already knew how to get his five-year old
sister to obey him: "Laïli, you bad girl, my father will be home
soon and you haven't even cleaned his spittoon! He's going to
be angry with you!" He also liked to show his little man's superiority when dealing with the dog, a huge beast whose ears and
tail had been clipped by my husband so he could participate in
dogfights. Laïli was terrified of him, but my little boy gave him
food right from his hand.

Family life had really improved since his birth. My husband
had bought carpets and musical instruments: the child was
bringing him luck, and we even rented a lovely house.

One evening, the little one began to have terrible diarrhea.
He was only two. The next day he was very sick. His father
took him to several mullahs, asking them to "expose his luck."
One *Saïd*,[8] the most important of them all, said: "If your son

---

[8] The *Saïds* are descendants of the prophet Mohammed. When villagers
meet them they kiss their hand as a sign of respect.

can hold on for forty days he will be saved, for he is exceptional; otherwise he will die."

The evening of the fortieth days he died, although the previous day it seemed he had started doing better.

I was sitting by his side, wanting to give him something to drink and hadn't realized that he was already dead, with his eyes open! Laïli screamed: "Oh, my brother!" I was yelling and tearing my hair out. When his father came home he understood right away what had happened; he clutched his belly and left the house without a word. My mother-in-law came running, as did the neighboring women who were lamenting with us. Then they took him away.[9]

My husband's shop went bankrupt and he lost everything. He was parading his grief everywhere and projected all his affection on Laïli: he would have a *gâdi*[10] come to the house and take her for rides through the city: "He isn't there anymore, she'll take his place."

For three years I had no other children and then a son again. Right away I called on the woman at whose place the previous one had died. She recited a verse from the Holy Koran and pierced the baby's ear and put a gold earring in it to protect him.

Then I had another son and two more daughters, may God be praised, and they were healthy. I have worked as a maid my whole life long, from about four or five in the morning, depending on the season, until ten or eleven at night. And I surely will keep working as long as my eyes can see and my hands and feet can obey me.

---

[9] Women do not attend funerals.
[10] A horse-drawn carriage.

The Story of Laïli, Nour Khânom's Daughter

My mother has been so unhappy because she married my
father, who was practically a stranger to her. She wasn't able
to get any support because she was far away from her family,
and alone from the start of her earliest childhood. She raised
all her children by herself; she taught us everything by telling
us about her life quite openly and explaining what examples to
follow and which to avoid. She never could eat or rest quietly
at home, first of all because of her in-laws and then because she
had so many children.

As is the custom, my brothers live in my father's house.
The oldest is unemployed and has six children. The youngest
left to try his luck in Iran, and the two others are civil servants. The family is getting deeper and deeper in debt all the
time, but we're not the only ones.[11] All that with a father who
has spent his life chasing skirts and gambling away the money
his wife was earning. Family life depended on her alone, but
she never had any say in the house. She was naive from the
start and has always been that way. If my father speaks, she is
silent. Unlike other women, she hasn't even gained in stature
by growing old.

My father devoted his youth to his mistresses. He would
bring them to the house and had them sleep on the same mattress as his wife, as if she didn't exist. I was very small when my
father would take me on rides and picnics with his friends. He
was well liked, for he knew how to be generous and he was a
good musician. At the time he was seeing a young girl from
Kabul who had been pregnant by him several times and had

---

[11]When a salary is just barely enough to buy food, the least little setback
causes a family's economy to falter. An illness, a debt of honor, the marriage of a son or the funeral of a father are all events that could put a man
in debt for a lifetime.

abortions; she was not Hazara. In the end, her mother managed to marry her off to another man because she was beautiful. My father would heap gifts upon his friends but never
concerned himself with my mother.

"You can do what you want," he would tell her. "It makes
no difference to me." She'd just cry. As she had nobody, no
brothers, no parents to support her and was used to being
mistreated, she'd say nothing. Not once did she ever reproach
him for anything whatsoever. I have heard her say: "If I speak,
he can reduce me to shreds. All I need to do is stay alive for my
children, and God will do with me as he sees fit."

Everybody gossiped. My father had proposed marriage
to that Kabul woman, but she had flatly refused him (I don't
know if that was because he was already married with children or because he was Hazara). He didn't insist. He would
go after girls in the family, married women—he was a handsome man. He would go and see them in the absence of their
husband, some cousin or other who didn't suspect any infidelity. These women knew that my mother wouldn't say anything. One of these has a daughter, one of her many children,
who resembles her uncle like two drops of water! Anyone
who would deny it is crazy: her face, her figure—it's my
father as a girl!

My mother's life was ghastly. When I look at her now, poor
thing, she is a very old woman at only sixty. She told me: "I'll
never give you to a young man. He'd be a womanizer just like
your father, and for you there'll be nothing but despair."

Soon it will be fifteen years since she married me off to an
old man. Too bad if he is poor; at least he won't make me lead a
dog's life and he'll be glad to be with me.

My earliest memory is a winter day when my brother had made
a snow lion just in front of our door. As I went out I fell over

that enormous thing with its huge red eyes; I was very small
and screamed out: *"Aïa, Aïa,*[12] something almost ate me!"

I also remember one time that I was at the bazaar. I came
to Ahengari in an alleyway of the blacksmiths' bazaar in Kabul.
A woman I didn't know had me come into her place. "Come
here, my dear!"

She was an aunt who had just divorced so that she could
marry again. She took me into a very dark house that smelled
bad. Inside, she tore some strips of curtain material to make a
doll for me (you put cotton around two bits of wood, shaped
like a cross, and tightly wrap this with bits of fabric). She put
iron bracelets on my wrists that were way too big for me. When
I came home, my mother forbade me to go back there, saying
that she was a "wicked woman."

When I was little, I had a very bad toothache one day. My
gums were all black and my breath smelled dreadful. They took
me to a wise woman who cried: "Thank God, your daughter is
still alive!" It was a *khamushak.* There are two kinds of illnesses:
one, *khamushak,* is male and can hit you all of a sudden and
be dangerous; the other is female and doesn't bother people.
Khamushak is a headache, a toothache, or a bellyache, and you
mustn't trust it. You should absolutely not go to a doctor, for
the medications he gives are "hot" and will only harm you.[13]

The woman gave us the name of a remedy to be picked up

---

[12]"Mother, Mother!"

[13]Laïli then gave me the list of hot and cold foods. Hot foods are black
tea, sugar, oil, garlic, pepper, meat, long-grain rice, fat, eggs, eggplant,
blackberries, raisins, jujubes, almonds, pistachios, nuts or fruit pits,
pomegranates, ripe grapes, mint, anise, cardamom, saffron.

Cold foods are other fruit such as green grapes, lemons and oranges,
potatoes, cucumbers, lettuce, carrots, short-grain rice, candied sugar,
corn, cow's milk, yogurt, whey, dry cheese made of cow's milk. "Cold
henna on your hair is good for quieting a headache," Laïli specified.

at the *atâr's.*[14] She recommended a diet that excluded oil, sugar, and fruit for two months. This woman was like a doctor; she knew every plant and every sickness. In the community she dealt with difficult births and the health problems of little ones. She often played the role of a *hâkim,*[15] which was extraordinary for they normally are men, specifically mullahs who have the power to give out *tawîz.* But it does happen that women with experience such as she and who have studied the Koran, take care of people, advise them, and give them talismans.

When I had these toothaches, one of my older brothers was responsible for watching us, my little brother and myself. He would put us to bed, saying that he was going to play outside. "Call me as soon as you wake up," he would say to me. He was always very sweet with me; he used to knit me sweaters and pants; he'd make dolls for me and miniature *liâf-e-sandali,*[16] and he'd play with us.

That day, when I woke up, he was far away playing with his ball. I called out: "Hassan Lâlâ, Hassan Lâlâ!"[17] But he couldn't hear us. When my mother came home from work at noon, the little one was crying and so was I. "Where is your brother?" she asked me. "He went to pee outside," I answered. I was afraid he'd be punished; my mother could hit hard. She went out and brought him back by the ear. She'd brought home a pot full of rice and sauce, and in her anger she threw it on the floor. Then she went to tear off a fistful of wild rose branches, had my brother get undressed, and beat him till he was bleeding. I begged her to stop, but she wouldn't. My toothache, my

---

[14]A pharmacist who prepares plant-based remedies and perfumes.
[15]A traditional doctor.
[16]A cover placed on top of the brazier.
[17]"Big brother Hassan!" Lâlâ is the name given to the oldest brother in the family.

mother in a rage, and my brother in tears—what a day! She went
back to work until ten o'clock at night. When she came home,
Hassan was in a bad way, I wasn't doing so well myself, and the
little one was hungry. She made food without a word and nursed
the baby. When my father asked why his son was in pain, we
didn't answer: we didn't want him to get angry with our mother.

When Hassan was feeling better, she sat down next to us to
comfort and sweet-talk us: "Your sister was sick and you just
left her, my boy. Stay home, close to them, and don't go hanging around the streets. I have to work elsewhere. While your
father is chasing ass, who will give you food to eat?"

She hit us a lot, but we always knew why.

I began working when I was eleven. In exchange for a kind
of stable where we all lived, one family employed both my
mother and me: she worked for one brother and I for the other
because their houses looked out onto the same courtyard. I
received forty afghani, that was nineteen years ago. I cleaned
the house, did the laundry, prepared the bread dough (one *sêr*
a day), and did a little cooking because I was clean, they said. I
did the dishes and tidied up. Sometimes we didn't come home
till eleven at night.

I was twelve when I got "sick"[18] for the first time. Of course,
no mother ever spoke of these kinds of things with her daughter:
sharm ast.[19] Since I had not been forewarned, I was crying and
wondering what was happening to me, how I had hurt myself.
But sensing that it shouldn't be discussed, I hid even from my

---

[18]Here *sick* refers to menstruation.

[19]*Sharm ast* is the expression that sums up everything that is embarrass-
ing to say or do, depending on whether it is taboo, shameful, or inconve-
nient. You do not speak of certain things, *sharm ast.* A girl doesn't laugh
in public, *sharm ast.* You don't smile at someone you do not know, *sharm
ast.* You don't call your husband, your uncles and aunts, or an older
woman by their first name, *sharm ast.*

mother to change and wash my clothes. There is shame in speaking of anything having to do with the female body: a woman will never state that she is pregnant, even if it is a topic of pride.

Our salaries were not sufficient for us and we left. I worked in a house for eighty afghani—the cost of living had risen enormously in two years. My mother did the laundry there. My father would go to Khanabad[20] and bring back rice to sell. He went bankrupt. A year later he wanted to sell carpets; this brought in nothing and he went back to getting rice again, which he would sell in Kabul after taking out the bits of stone and dust. He was always losing money. He returned to the country to grow crops, but he couldn't stand life in the countryside anymore and came back to Kabul, this time to settle down with *kohna-forushi*.[21]

I was never unemployed. In the beginning I used to do housework and another woman would do the cooking. She was a Pashtun from Kandahar; orphaned, she had grown up in this house to which she returned with her three boys after her husband died.[22] She was repulsive and never combed her hair;

---

[20]A city east of Kunduz in the north of Afghanistan, about two hundred kilometers from Kabul.

[21]Literally "where old goods are sold." Batches of old clothing from Europe or the United States are bought up by wholesale merchants from Kandahar, who resell them to small retailers in Kabul. The latter get together in groups in several huge flea markets where shoes are repaired, sweaters are taken apart, and an enormous choice of clothing is offered, either completely new or patched up.

[22]As in Arab countries, it is not unusual that young children, boys or girls, are taken in by a family in which they have the standing of poor relatives or "servants." Thus, in the house there is often a family in the greater sense of the term, which includes not only the parents and children with their offspring, but also the family of the servants, who are fed and clothed.

she also smoked the *tchilam*[23] and this tears up your throat. She was a bit crazy, but the family had taken her in. Very quickly they asked my mother to let me do their cooking.

Gradually I learned, thanks to the daughters of the family, who all participated in making the dough when there were guests. What a happy feeling in the kitchen! We'd prepare *bolâni,*[24] *âshak,*[25] and *qâbuli.*[26] I was busy every minute.

The sky was still full of stars in the winter when I would get up at five in the morning. I'd go out to get meat—there is much greater choice very early in the morning, and the meat was still nice looking—and one or two *sêr* of wood that I'd carry in my arms all the way to the house. I prepared the *yakhni*[27] and then run to clean one or two of the rooms. I set the breakfast table; they would get up and I served tea. I polished shoes. As soon as I was done with that I'd go back to my stove. With half the meal cooked, I'd go and sweep another room. Barely would I have my hands on the onions and rice and I would hear the voice of the master of the house: "Little one, go get me my suit from the closet!" By the time I came back to the kitchen my onions were burned.

"Damn that madwoman, why doesn't she do anything?"

"You do everything better than she does," they'd tell me. They liked me a lot.

Two years later they moved and suggested that we come with them. But that took us too far away from my brothers' school, and so we had to leave them.

That was the moment that Mina's[28] father appeared. I was

---

[23] Waterpipe.

[24] Large loaves of bread baked in fat and stuffed with vegetables.

[25] A kind of very light macaroni in a spicy sauce with a sour cheese base.

[26] One of many ways of preparing Afghan rice.

[27] Boiled meat to be eaten with rice.

[28] Laïli's oldest daughter.

fourteen. He was a relative of my father's who had divorced his wife because he realized she had a lover (I since learned that this was the woman I had met at the bazaar when I was small). He then went in search of adventure in Pakistan and India—I was two at the time! After an absence of twelve years he returned.

When he saw me, he asked my father, "Say, who is that pretty flower growing in your garden?"

He fell in love with me. I was fourteen and he was twenty years older. I thought I'd go mad: I walked in the snow with bare feet, I even swallowed medications hoping to die. One month later we were engaged; my mother was pleased that he was older than I. At the time I was in love with a cousin who lived on the same courtyard as we: we'd talk, laugh, tell each other stories, play cards. My brother was furious: "You shouldn't see him or talk to him: you're not children anymore!"

He was perpetually watching me, forbidding me to be out in public or use makeup. My cousin wanted to talk to my father and ask for permission to marry me, but I was so ashamed to be a topic of discussion that I urged him to keep quiet.

Once engaged, I saw my cousin, who reproached me for having accepted the old man. I cried because there was nothing I could do; I had not been told before the engagement, and he cried with me. He proposed that I become his mistress, but I refused: my life would be lost if I accepted that, and so would the honor of my brothers.

My fiancé was very jealous and would follow me everywhere: if I went to put a pot on the fire, he'd be behind me; if I were carrying water, there he was again. He exasperated and frightened me at the same time. It was then that he beat me for the first and last time: his aunt told him I had a boyfriend. "When she scratches her head, she is saying hello to him. When she strokes her face, she is sending him a kiss . . ."

It made him crazy. Since he had neither home nor family,

he was living in my father's house. We all slept in the same
room: my father, my mother, my brothers and their wives,
and the unmarried children. I slept close to my mother. In the
middle of the night, he'd come and talk to me. I'd wrap myself
tightly in my dress so that he wouldn't touch me. "Show me
your face," he'd say, "and don't cry or that will mean you have
another lover!"

One night he slapped me. My father woke up and defended
me: "You are old and I have given you my daughter who is very
young. She knows nothing about life. Marry her, take her with
you, and don't even let a dog inside your house so you can hide
the fact that you have a pretty wife."

The night of our wedding he understood that I was chaste
and suddenly he changed his attitude; he became kind and
trusting toward me. And yet, I have never loved him.

Just before my marriage, I was working for the new owners
of the apartment we were renting. The wife was very young,
and we had a lot of fun together all day long. I'd finish my
work quickly, and we'd sit down and play cards or music while
we danced with a tambourine. When my mother saw us, she
criticized the young woman: "*Bîbî Shirîn,*[29] what you're doing
there is not good: my daughter is like a country girl. Since you
are an excellent seamstress, teach her to sew, to embroider, to
do hems."

I didn't have any days off (when you are part of a family a
day off makes no sense!), but they took me everywhere they
went, visiting or taking walks. My fiancé didn't like seeing me
work outside the house. I left them. The seven months preced-
ing my wedding I stayed home, watched over by my brother,
like a properly raised girl. At night I could sleep only at my
father's house. For celebrations, the family dragged me around

---

[29] *Bîbî* is a title given to a woman as a sign of respect.

to go visiting. I was coquettish and they didn't trust me. Then came the wedding day.

The evening of my wedding day, my mother didn't dare say anything to me. We went to the toilet and all she did was hand me a white sheet, without a word, on the sly, so that nobody would see us. At the time I had no girlfriends with whom I could talk. My sister Gol-Begom, who is ten years younger than I and had just got married, had learned many things on her own about marriage and women's problems. And my brother, who was horrible with me and wouldn't allow me to see anyone, has calmed down with our younger sisters, whom he leaves totally alone. As she gave me the sheet, the only thing my mother said to me was, "Don't worry about it, little one, it's the same thing for every girl; you just have to get through it . . ."

I didn't understand a word of what she said, and then I heard her say to my husband: "Be very careful, you're old and you've been married before. My daughter is young, don't kill her tonight!"

They closed the door.

My husband asked me to get undressed but, crying, I refused. "It doesn't matter, but you can't stay like that until tomorrow morning. You know that all the women in the family are waiting in the next room. Everybody is already saying that you're not a virgin anymore since we've been living in the same house. Come on now, get undressed!"

He was so old and I so young, why did we have to sleep together? I asked him to turn off the light. I was terrified. I cried out a little when he came close to me. "You've got to be quiet, everyone's going to hear you!"

That night I suffered more than with any of my deliveries, as if someone had stuck a knife in my belly. For a week I couldn't bear his coming close to me or even talking to me: I loathed him. But since the wedding night when he found out

that I was a virgin, my husband has always been very good
to me.

Since I had no father-in-law in whose house to live, we
stayed with my parents. All of us in the same room. There were
just too many people around. We'd wait till the others were
asleep, and when my husband would come close I'd weep with
shame, thinking my father or brothers could hear us. It's always
been done on the sly as if it were forbidden or immoral, like
thievery.

My first five children were born at home, in my father's
house; I now have seven of them, and I know nothing about
life.[30]

Still, I'm lucky to have a serious and good husband. He
has never taken me by force; when I wasn't in the mood, he
would accept that without getting angry. When I reached the
sixth month of pregnancy he wouldn't touch me until two
months after the birth. But not all men are like that; it's quite
unusual, in fact. My brothers' wives have complained to me.
"If I refuse," they say, "he swears at me and asks what kind of
a husband I want, someone younger than he, of course, if he
himself doesn't suit me!"

And all of them give in to their husbands.

Two months after the wedding I was pregnant with my first
child but didn't know it. I was hurting everywhere and itch-
ing terribly all over. The women around me were blaming my
mother for having neglected me. "She must have been drinking
cold water. When you prepared the wedding bedroom, it surely
wasn't clean enough!"

My mother was upset but said nothing. This went on
for three months and then gradually my belly began to get
rounder, and I understood the situation at the same time that

---

[30]Laïli was not yet thirty at this time.

the others did. I kept regretting the marriage that was deforming me and making me sick.

They took me to the maternity clinic for the delivery.

Next to me was a woman having her eighth child, twisting and turning and screaming with pain. The nurses threatened her: "If you move we'll operate on you!"

What a racket! It was so terrifying that I escaped to go home and have the baby there! My husband was away doing his military service. Originally, when he was called up he was abroad because of his wife. My brother alerted him of his son's birth by letter and organized a magnificent *shao e shash*[31] for the entire family. For once I didn't do a thing, because I was *zatsha*.[32] So the family came together and we chose the name of the boy: each person in the group wrote or had someone write a name on a piece of paper and then there was a drawing. The name that came out was the one my father had chosen, and we called the child Azîz.[33]

I started back to work again. I left the baby with my sister-in-law, but she became sick. With the children and the family problems I couldn't keep a steady job for very long. One time, I worked in a house where the manservant was a thief. The police came. It was the home of foreigners, and they asked me why I was working there; it wasn't a place for a young Afghan woman to be. Another time, one of my children was doing stupid things because there wasn't anyone to watch him. Once, I rented a house separate from my father, but I came back to him when I was out of work and had no money to pay the rent.

My husband did nothing and would watch the children as long as he wasn't out looking for work. He tried a whole slew

---

[31]The newborn is celebrated on the sixth night after its birth.
[32]Recovering from childbirth.
[33]The Beloved.

of little jobs, but none of them brought in any money. He even worked in Iran and came back with a transistor and just enough money to pay back the debts he'd incurred to buy his passport.

My fifth boy was three years old when I became pregnant again. One Friday when I came home from work (I worked even on Fridays), I found the house empty because my husband had taken the children for a walk. The next night my youngest son woke me up: "Hopa,[34] I have a headache!"

He had a terrible fever, but in the morning I had to go to work. By the evening he was burning up. My brother was furious and asked why I hadn't taken him to the doctor. If I were to take them there whenever they had a bit of fever, I'd be spending my days and all my money there. My brother gave me enough to pay the doctor, who gave me a prescription, saying that it was no more than a cold and a sore throat. I went back to work. The next evening he was completely paralyzed. We had to go back to the hospital. Taking the child in his arms, my husband suggested we go by taxi to get there faster. I refused just to save the thirty afghanis the taxi would cost and to bring home a bit of meat for the soup. "Let's take the bus, it will be just as fast and for only two afghanis." Always poverty on my mind, and it made me act like an idiot. It was crowded in the bus; carrying his son in his arms, my husband was not aware that someone was stealing the thirty-five hundred afghanis my father had lent him. When we came home, they asked what the doctor had said. I started to cry, and my husband said the little boy was paralyzed. It was as if he said he had died. My two sisters were crying, my brothers moaning, and so were the other children. My father told us to take him to a mullah to have him "expose his luck." "Do you have any money?" he asked my husband. "Yes, uncle, the money you gave me!"

---

[34]"Mamma."

As he put his hand in his pocket he quickly understood he'd been robbed. "So much for the money," my father said. "Your son needs to get better. It is difficult to make a man, making money is easy . . ."

The mullah said the child had fallen and must have been afraid; his *tawîz* would do him no good. "Just cut his hair." Then the foreign woman for whom I was working at the time took us to another doctor, who gave the little one a shot in his spine and told us he had polio.

His limbs were hard as wood, and he could neither speak nor eat. They gave him massages at the hospital. I was six months pregnant and brought him there every day. He began to move his arms and feet a bit and started to talk again. My father advised me to keep him in a dark room and feed him pigeon meat. We tried that for five days, but he refused to take any food. Then he very slowly began to make some progress. No Afghan doctor ever told us poor people to have children vaccinated. After my son's polio, I took my little ones to the hospital myself to get them vaccinated. I soon knew what was going on: they'd give twenty vaccinations with the same needle, the best way to pass on any disease! And then, too, they frightened us by refusing to explain anything at all. The idea of going to the hospital terrifies people.

I should be going to Mazar for my little cripple, to the *ziârat* of Ali.[35] I've been told that he'd get better, but when will I find the time to go there?

At the ziârat women always have a wish they want fulfilled.

---

[35] A *ziârat* is the tomb of a holy man where women gather, normally on Wednesdays. It is one of the rare occasions to go out to the hammam and on family visits. The "*ziârat* of Ali" is in the great mosque of Mazar-i-Sharif. Ali, the cousin and son-in-law of the Prophet, is Islam's fourth caliph.

One would like her son to pass his exams, another cannot have children, a third has only girls and wants a boy. But it is also a place where women get together and talk about their problems. It is a favorite place for gossiping.

I had five sons and wanted a daughter—I went there seven Wednesdays in a row with a cousin who was hoping for a son. The eighth Wednesday I prepared a *halwâ*[36] that I brought along in a pot for those who live close to the ziârat,[37] candles, millet for the pigeons, and a hundred afghanis for the guardian of the tomb. I prayed as I wept with emotion and then I went home. Mina was born, though my cousin didn't have the same luck: she had a girl ten months later. But a year after Mina, I was pregnant again, and now it was a little too much!

I had the daughter I had wished for and didn't want any more. I had made the decision to have an operation and my husband agreed; but my little girl wasn't four months old yet when the new baby made itself known. And yet, I had tried to take the pill they advise us to use when you leave the maternity clinic. My legs immediately became painful and swollen, my belly blew up, too, and I was nauseated; I quickly threw in the towel. In any case, I didn't have any time to think about it this time. I was nursing my little girl and another was on the way! I decided to get rid of it.

I began to swallow just about any drug. Neighbors of mine suggested several of them that made me desperately sick, but nothing happened. A cousin told me to put a kind of plant "in there" that grows on the edge of the *djouï:*[38] its leaves swell up

---

[36]A brown dough of flour and fat, to which water and sugar are added. It is also distributed to neighbors during celebrations.

[37]Generally holy men, guardians of the tomb, or a *malang,* a wandering hermit who lives off the donations of the faithful.

[38]An irrigation canal in the country, more of a ditch.

and that helps the fetus to come down. But I was afraid to die, something that has happened more than once to a woman—those plants are full of bacteria. I preferred to go and see a dâî; surely she would find a solution.

She asked me for five hundred afghanis and set to work. First she gave me a potion of her own making to drink. Then she had me lie down flat on my belly on the ground, on top of a bowl placed at the level of my lower abdomen. She climbed on my back and walked on my kidneys, hoping to set the child loose: it was horrible! I had more pain than when I gave birth, but thank God I am still alive. She was very well known, however, and I know that several unmarried girls had dealings with her. But for me nothing she tried worked: eight months later a second daughter was born and God is merciful, for she is four years old now.[39]

After her birth I asked to have the operation at last. Few men allow it: what will become of them if they can no longer prove their virility? Often the women themselves are hesitant. They're afraid of the hospital, and for religious reasons they are very judgmental of those who do have the operation. "You wanted to have it done; heaven has punished you: your son became ill and you had two daughters, one right after the other!"

Believe me, in spite of what people say, I'm quite happy with it! And the second little girl is so sweet! One of my sisters-in-law would like to do it as well, but she's had so many children (she's expecting her tenth!) that she is too weak and afraid she might die during the operation. What would her children do without a mother?

Mullahs predict the future—I was supposed to have twelve

---

[39]They don't say that a child is handsome or healthy—that would entice the evil eye.

children, mostly sons. I have five boys and two girls and no
more chance of having any others, thank God!

Just like the talismans, destiny is in the hands of mullahs.
The tawîz contain sacred formulas that do good or heal a sick
person; handling the *djâdou*[40] is more delicate.

First of all, a mullah always refuses to put a curse on anything, but a small sum of money can be enough to convince
some of them. Women come to ask for their husband's trust
and love. One may complain of her older sister-in-law and
wants her brother to divorce; another one may want to get rid
of an intolerable mother-in-law. The mullah writes the names
of the woman and the one she wishes to affect on an egg with
saffron; he also writes the request. Then the egg is washed and
the formula is dissolved in the water that, somehow or other,
they get the targeted person to drink. Sometimes, they pierce a
piece of fat with needles in a bit of paper you must hide under
the pillow or in the clothes of your enemy, and even if that
poor creature goes to every doctor in the world, they wouldn't
be able to heal him. For example, my cousin's husband was
in good health, able to support a large family. Lovely in company, he was hideous to his wife, whom he beat up regularly.
Someone put a curse on him, and from one day to the next he
went insane. People suspect that my cousin went to a mullah to
bring some calm into her life. Now the poor man goes raving
through the streets and, like a beggar, picks up anything at all
to put in his shirt.

Another woman was unhappy with her husband. One day
her parents noticed traces of egg yolk on the wall of her bedroom. They understood that the family-in-law had gone to see
a mullah to hurt their daughter. Right away, the father went to
see another one who gave him an amulet to ward off the bad

---

[40]Magic spells.

fortune, and he brought his daughter home with him. A few days later, the husband came to reclaim his wife. He threw his family out of the house, and since then they are quite happy together.

My brother was married when he was fourteen to an older girl. On the wedding night he was incapable of performing his duty. They took him to a mullah who declared that someone clearly had put a curse on him.[41] He wrote a formula on three eggs, which my brother had to eat three days in a row. Then, still with saffron, he put an inscription on the blade of an ax and having heated it in the fire, he asked the boy to urinate on it . . . And he was fine.

As for me, I have now been married for fifteen years. Sometimes when the children are asleep I am alone with their father. I ask him if he's under the impression that he has a wife. "You're there, aren't you?" he answers. And what about me? I have a husband, but what difference does it make? One day follows another and they're all the same. I was young and now it's all over; I've gotten nothing out of it. Although he loves me and has always been kind to me, I have simply grown used to him. Even now, the cousin I used to love comes to see me. He says: "How are you, my dear? You've grown so old!" He has asked me every now and then to be his, but I always answer that until now I have been a decent woman and I plan to stay that way. I like him a lot, and just seeing him puts me in a good mood. In the beginning my husband was very jealous of him. I warned him: "If you want me to be bad, just tie my feet. I may talk and laugh with this or that cousin, but my heart is pure!" When I come home, even if it's late, my husband smiles at me and always welcomes me warmly.

---

[41]If he suffered from impotence the young man would have to accept being divorced and dishonored.

It must be said that when we were married our entire
fortune consisted of a mattress and a blanket; by working hard
we have gradually managed to buy what is absolutely necessary. I never blame my husband for his inactivity. My neighbor
is always astounded: "How can you stand it, and you don't
say anything to him?" What would be the point? Arguments
wouldn't improve my life. That's the way it is, and all I can do
is go on.

In the morning I get up early to take the bread dough to the
baker. Then I come back quickly to straighten up the house.
The children wake up, they have to be fed before school. I put
on my chador and go off to work. When I come home in the
evening, the house is hell: the little ones cling to me, one is
sick, the others are fighting. I sew, I patch; I am barely sitting
down when the youngest ones want to go to sleep—I get their
mattresses ready, tuck in the blankets, stroke them . . . In a life
like this there is no time to go out. I only go out for a wedding,
to visit someone who is sick, or for a death in the family. Celebrations don't bring any rest to women, but rather additional
worries about cooking, dishes, and housework. Soon it will be
the *Aïd e Qorban:*[42] we Shiites must make sure that everything
on our bodies and in our homes is perfectly scrubbed. Women
clean from top to bottom, from the windowpanes to the hand-
kerchiefs. One evening before the Aïd we cook the halwâ,
which we will then distribute as an offering among our neighbors and to the poor in the street. When relatives come to visit,
we are obliged to feed them, and too simple a meal would put
the hosts in a bad light: "They can't afford it!" And that would
be a disgrace for sure.

---

[42]The feast of sacrificing the sheep to commemorate Abraham's sacrifice.
It is the time when those who can afford it go on pilgrimage to Mecca,
which allows them to use the title *hadj*.

Now I am off on Fridays; but I still get up early because the day is always full. I wash myself and the children from top to toe; it's the only day that I have the time for that. Then I do the laundry because tomorrow they go back to school. A little housework, a little cooking, and soon the day is over, exhausting, without any pleasures or diversion.

Every other Friday I go to the hammam. My two oldest ones, who are now more than ten, go there with their father. I bring some of the others, and my little sister takes care of the rest.[43] I can't go to the hammam every week; it would cost too much. On that day, at five in the morning, I take my daughters by the hand to wait my turn and get a cabin. In the common room there is a basin with hot water and one with cold water. It gets dirty quickly, and I prefer having a cabin so that my little girls won't get sick.

I bring along a bowl, soap, a brush, pumice stone, a massage glove, a comb, and a towel. A cabin costs more than the common room, but my sons who aren't ten yet can come with us; they're not allowed to go into the room where women are naked down to the waist. The cabin is a tiny little tiled room with just one hot-water faucet and one cold. We start by cleaning our feet very thoroughly to dissolve the dirt; I scrub the girls and we rub ourselves clean with the massage glove; finally, we wash our hair with the *guel e sar shuï*.[44] The hammam has customers every day, but on Fridays there's a mob: Thursday nights is when we have relations with our husband. So as long

---

[43]Nasrîn, fifteen, has been living with her sister for a long time. She has the role of Laïli's oldest daughter and takes care of the children when their mother is at work. It is their mother who made this decision: she "gave" Nasrîn to Laïli, who feeds her, dresses her, and gets her trousseau together—this is her responsibility.

[44]A kind of clay that is used as shampoo.

as you haven't washed you are impure and therefore can't go to
pray. That is why you use water over your entire body.[45] Hence
the classic jokes of the hammam: "Oh, my dear, you must have
slept with your husband if you're here now!" And the other
one will answer that nobody can prove this, and then everyone
bursts out laughing.

For one year there was a woman who lived around the same
courtyard as we; she was still young and married to her first
cousin. They had eight children. Usually, she was dressed normally and worked at home. Some days, she would go around
all made up and with her hair done, dressed as if for a wedding.
In the evening, when her husband came home, she'd sit in a
corner of the room like a new bride while her fifteen-year-old
daughter prepared the meal, washed the dishes, and took care
of the younger ones. The next day, we'd see them washing up
in torrents of water; a hot day, a cold day, nothing escaped the
neighbors! With my brother, who'd been noticing the same
routine, I'd laugh so hard I couldn't breathe. The woman, in
full bloom, was marvelous, round with a huge bottom. Her
poor husband, exhausted from all this ardor, for he worked
from morning to night, was as skinny as they come! His feet
were as thin as skewers. "Don't eat so much!" I sometimes told
her.[46] "What are you talking about?" she'd answer, playing the
innocent. No doubt she was lucky enough to know what I have
never known. I am like a beast of burden, doing everything
out of habit, work, children . . . Even debts no longer worry
me, they're part of our life. But nothing to show for it, many
children: my life is bitter.

Gol-Begom, my sister who is twenty, had an easier childhood. She just married a cousin who is twenty-three, and she

---

[45]Koran, suras 4:43 and 5:6.
[46]"Eating" means having sexual relations.

loves him. Her father-in-law, our uncle, was very strict with the women in his house; he's becoming more tolerant and allows her to go out.

For Nasrîn, the youngest one, things will go better. She has a hell of a will and states out loud that nobody will ever make her put on a chador. I wore one at the age of twelve! But she's been more spoiled than we were because I was the one who raised her.

My two little girls are three and five. What future do they have? Their grandfather grumbles when he sees them in short skirts with just their little underpants and no long pants like we wore. But their father doesn't care. When an older person comes to the house, we dress the little girls in long pants and cover their arms; but for us it no longer makes any sense and we raise them differently. In any case, they'll go all the way through school and they'll choose their own husbands and their own professions. They'll be free to go out, go to the movies, but "decently," for that is what is important: to be pure of heart.

Of course, we are poor people; but whatever I can do for their happiness, to make them into happier women than we are, I will do.

I have faithfully transcribed the story of Laïli and her mother, and my heart aches.

I wanted to stick as closely as possible to Laïli's narrative just the way she told it to me because I used to take great joy in listening to her and having her lay bare what life in its most intimate details was like for families of very few means.

She was very good, too, at describing the environment, the games, and the psychic world of a small and poor Afghan girl in the sixties and the society's slow evolution before a twenty-three-year-long war tore the country to pieces. What strikes me now is to find in her words again that mixture of fatalism and superstition, but also of common sense and strength that surprised us so much in Afghanistan. The contemptible passages about the behavior of Nour Khânom's husband or mother-in-law only confirm that cruelty within a family can have the same face as anywhere else with just one difference—and it is a fundamental one: in Nour Khânom's case there was no outside help in her struggle against the hostile treatment she was forced to suffer.

In 1978, I could tell from the delight shining from Laïli's face that her family had chosen the side of the Communists. Obviously, she herself did not belong to any party. But she told me that her brothers had been militant for some time, and they were all expecting a great deal from the new regime that was in the process of settling in: more equality, more hope for poor people and for the women of Afghanistan. Then, too, some of the ministers in the government of that spring of 1978 had lived in houses just like hers, with cardboard instead of glass in the windows to protect against the cold and ten people in one room, like the poor: surely they of all people would know what poverty was!

But when I left her in December 1978, she was troubled and uncertain. The Afghan Communists had been wrangling among themselves only one month after the coup d'état. Her brothers had been arrested, and she had had no news of them since then. Where, in the end, were the changes she had been dreaming about?

In 1979, Laïli's oldest son, then a young soldier changing the guard at the entrance to the Lycée Esteqlal, was accidentally killed by a bullet from his own Kalashnikov whose trigger he had pressed.

Laïli was killed in the bombings that steeped Kabul in blood when the Communists departed. I don't know the date or the exact circumstances of her death, nor who else vanished with her on that day. I didn't hear about it until 1994, by chance, when I met someone who had known her.

I still see her as if she were standing before me. Her Asiatic black eyes, her lively and always somewhat laughing look, her lovely bright smile with the little gap between her upper teeth, "teeth of happiness." Her braided hair and the automatic gesture with which she'd push back the green tulle veil that would always slide down over her head as soon as she made any motion. The dress with its bright red and green flowers, its rounded neckline and long sleeves, tight in the waist, which she wore over full white nylon pants, embroidered at the bottom. Her feet most of the time in plastic sandals, yellow, blue, green, or pink, bought at the bazaar for a few pennies. The little vest, beautifully embroidered, that she would don on days of celebration. Her hands with their henna-dyed nails. Her burst of laughter when she put on the chador that would hide her from the stares of men on her way back home. Her glow, her intelligence, her curiosity for everything I could tell her about our life, the life we led in France, where women have as many rights as men. I mourn for her, as I do for everyone I have loved.

Pashtun Women Speak

Laïli, who never learned to read or write, had told me her life in its daily details with remarkable good sense and intelligence.

Shirîn, daughter of a *khân*[1] and a *Saïd,* from one of those privileged circles that had both wealth and an honorable rank, provided me with invaluable documentation as well.

Pashtun, she was thirty-seven when we spent time together in Kabul. She was the mother of three boys, cultured and highly refined—modern and feminist, though careful to respect certain traditions that, in her eyes, gave Afghan culture its value—she gave me her critical view of the condition of women in Afghanistan. Ardently Muslim, she enlightened me on the true place of women in the sacred texts.

Laïli and Shirîn have different levels of consciousness. Belonging to social classes that are disconnected in every way, one still finds one thing that unites them: the same claim to dignity, to that "purity" that is the honor of Afghan women.

---

[1]The *khân* is a country lord.

Shirîn's Reflections on the Texts of the Holy Koran[2]

The Koran led to a veritable revolution in seventh-century[3] Arab society, specifically where the women of that period were concerned.

It is all too often forgotten that the first believer in our religion was a woman—Khadija—the first wife of the Prophet, fifteen years his senior, who would buy back slaves in the marketplaces to set them free. It is to her that we owe the first soldiers of Islam as well as Fatima, the Prophet's favorite daughter.

Mohammed always spoke about improving women's lot, protecting them by giving them social status. It is according to the data of what was current in seventh-century Arab culture that the status of women in the texts of the holy Koran should be seen and the deeper meaning be drawn, which is respect and tolerance.

In the pre-Islamic Arab world, newborns of the female gender were sometimes buried:

> *When if one of them receiveth tidings of the birth of a*
> *   female,*
> *his face remaineth darkened, and he is wroth inwardly.*
> *He hideth himself from the folk because of the evil of that*
> *   whereof*
> *he hath had tidings, (asking himself): Shall he keep it in*
> *   contempt,*
> *or bury it beneath the dust. Verily evil is their judgment.*
> *(16:58–59)*

---

[2] The following passages are from *The Meaning of the Glorious Koran*, trans. Mohammed Marmaduke Pickthall (New York: Meridian, 1997).
[3] The Hegira, the Prophet's departure for Medina, marks the first year of the Muslim calendar, in the year 622 C.E.

Elsewhere it is said that girls and boys are gifts of God (42:49).

If one reads in the sacred texts that to men women are like their earth (2:223), this is far from being pejorative, for it gives an essential value to the woman: the earth bears the fruit that is necessary to life and therefore man treats it with care and respect. This is the attitude recommended to the faithful to have toward their wife, as is honesty and equity in problems of misunderstanding, repudiation, and inheritance (2, 4, 24), generosity, and purity.

During the era of the Prophet, women had no possibility whatsoever to provide themselves with clothing or food; they were entirely dependent on men. During periods of war, they became widows and orphans, and, unable to meet their needs, all they could do was to be sold like cattle.

The Koran commands men to take responsibility for women as human beings and—there is a tendency to forget this condition that is, nevertheless, quite explicit in the texts— to treat them equitably:

> *And if ye fear that ye will not deal fairly by the orphans,*
> *Marry of the women, who seem good to you, two or three*
> *Or four; and if ye fear that ye cannot do justice (to so many)*
> *Then one only or the captives that your right hands possess.*
> *Thus it is more likely that ye will not do injustice. (4:3)*

Thirteen hundred years later, there are no "captives of war" any longer, and the conditions of life have changed for men; thus what remains is the deeper meaning of the text, the de- mand for integrity. Today, the reasons for having several wives are no longer the same: it is no proof of generosity anymore but rather the fact of taking advantage of women as cattle. Only wealthy proprietors, a few mullahs, or old men can afford multiple wives, and it is actually condemned by the popular wisdom that states that "a man who has two wives does not breathe comfortably." "One piece of wood does not make a fire, but two wives do not make a home."

Everything that is essential in the religion has never been said for man alone but for all women and men, who are equal before God:

> *Wed not idolatresses till they believe; for lo! a believing*
> *bondwoman is better than an idolatress though she please*
> *you; and give not your daughters in marriage to idolaters*
> *till they believe, for lo! a believing slave is better than an*
> *idolater though he please you. (2:221)*

It will be noted that they often say that women may only marry Muslims, whereas men have the right to take a Jew or Christian as a wife. Yet, the Prophet was careful always to draw a parallel between men and women.

If a man is guilty he will be punished the same way a woman is. Adultery, which assaults a society founded on the family, is considered to be a crime:

> *The adulterer and the adulteress, scourge ye each one of*
> *them (with) a hundred stripes. And let not pity for the*
> *twain withhold you from obedience to Allah, if ye believe*
> *in Allah and the Last Day. And let a party of believers*
> *witness their punishment. (24:2)*

But the following verses quickly warn those who might want to rush into accusing a woman:

> *And those who accuse honorable women but bring not four*
> *witnesses, scourge them with eighty stripes and never*
> *afterward accept their testimony—They indeed are evildoers—*
> *And it shall avert the punishment from her if she bear witness*
> *before Allah four times that the thing he saith is indeed false,*

And a fifth time that the wrath of Allah be upon her if he
speaketh truth. (24:4, 8, 9)

This comes down to stating that no one may sit in judgment
upon others.

To attain purity and greater spiritual strength through chastity
is not a monopoly of Islam. Here, too, however, the commandments are directed at men (24:30) as well as at women, who
should no longer be prey to male lust:

O Prophet! Tell thy wives and thy daughters and the women
of the believers to draw their cloaks close round them (when
they go abroad). That will be better, that so they may
be recognized and not annoyed. Allah is ever Forgiving,
Merciful. (33:59)

Love and kindness must unite man and woman:

They are raiment for you and ye are raiment for them. (2:187)

And of his Signs is this:

He created for you helpmeets from yourselves that ye
might find rest in them, and He ordained between you
love and mercy. (30:21)

Men and women are equal before God:

Lo! men who surrender unto Allah, and women who
surrender, and men who believe and women who believe,
and men who obey and women who obey, and men who
speak the truth and women who speak the truth, and men
who persevere in righteousness and women who persevere,
and men who are humble and women who are humble,
and men who give alms and women who give alms, and men
who fast and women who fast, and men who guard their

*modesty and women who guard their modesty, and men who
remember Allah much and women who remember—Allah
hath prepared for them forgiveness and a vast reward. (33:35)*

It just so happens that Islamic law has always been in the
hands of men who have interpreted it one way only, emphasiz-
ing the texts that suited them. Customs have taken root that
way, and so has the consciousness of women.

When the law reducing the "marriage price" to three
hundred afghanis came out in 1978, jokes sprang up all over:
"Three hundred afghanis! I can buy myself a wife a day!" This
proves that they were completely unaware of the basic problem,
namely, the disgrace of selling daughters.

Few Muslims understand the great principles of the Koran.
Everyone knows the concrete precepts, but the profound wisdom of the text is based on divine mercy. The Koran enhanced
the prestige of the Arab woman of the seventh century as a
human person, and the believers of the twentieth century claim
to base themselves on sacred texts in order to treat women like
inferior beings!

It seems to me that, in contrast to the Judeo-Christian
civilizations that had power in the world, those coming out of
Islam had hardly any means to evolve in the course of the thirteen and a half centuries of their history. Always under attack
in their identity as subjugated or colonized peoples, Muslim
cultures seem to have found support by teaching the rules of
everyday life and have become almost ossified just to survive.
Afghanistan, a mountainous country where the austerity of
life fit well into the framework of Islam's stringency, was one of
the first to be converted, and it was to the cry of "Allah Akbar"
that Afghan warriors repelled the army of the British Empire
in the nineteenth century. It is the same cry the inhabitants of
Kabul uttered, women and men alike, perched on the rooftops

and terraces of their homes, one Thursday evening in February
1979, just after the Soviet invasion.

> *And women have rights similar to those of men over*
> *them in kindness, and men are a degree above them.*
> *Allah is Mighty, Wise. (2:228)*

Because of his natural superiority, then, man supposedly has the
right to dominate woman. The theory is not peculiar to Islam, and
everyone knows that it is found worldwide. In one place it takes
the form of machismo; somewhere else it is sexual harassment or
slavery. There are examples of sexism in every country and in almost
every culture.

My student and friend Nadjib insisted, in 1978, that the misery
of Afghan women was directly connected to that of men and that
it was basically the same problem—poverty and lack of education.
It should be clearly recognized that the situation of a poor rural
woman and that of a woman in Kabul raised in an upper-class family have nothing in common.

Shîrin's Story

I spent my whole childhood in the Kumar Valley, northeast of
Jalalabad. My father, a tribal chief, was an extraordinary man.
He admired my mother, a refined and cultured person, and
often asked her advice, sometimes even had her write some of
his letters. She died very young, and I hardly knew her.

Like all the girls in our families, and the boys as well, of
course, I learned to read and write at the mosque, where a
mullah taught us Persian and Pashtun literature, the holy
Koran, Arabic grammar, and the exegesis of sacred texts.

My father had married another woman, but he was

especially attentive to my education. When there was a meeting at our house—I was maybe twelve or thirteen—he would ask me to attend so that I could learn something. "Speak," he'd say, "and I shall listen to your opinion!" Elsewhere, girls were not allowed to join the men and even less to open their mouths; in contrast, my father urged me to do so, and I certainly didn't miss a chance!

From twelve on, at puberty, I had to wear the chador when I went out. Peasant women go to the fields with their faces uncovered, but my father had rank, and his prestige would have suffered if he had allowed his women to be seen like any other woman.

They say that the appearance of the chador in Afghanistan goes back to the era of King Habibollah, who kept more than two hundred women in his harem.[4] The more women one has, the harder it is to watch them, according to a popular saying. Therefore, a way had to be found to make malicious gossips stop their talking: a veil that would hide women completely to the point that, dressed in this ghostly outfit, one could no longer tell the servants from the princesses as they were coming and going outside the palace. I don't know whether the tale is true, but in any event, in the fifties, the aristocratic women and those of the bourgeoisie only wore the chador in the cities.

This makes me think of something the last "fiancée" of King Habibollah told me:

"He knew that my mother, the concubine of one of his ministers, had been very beautiful. He summoned me the day I turned fifteen to take a look at me. Sadness pervaded the whole house as if it were in mourning, but my uncle explained that, since it was the king's pleasure, we had to submit to it. The ap-

---

[4]Habibollah reigned from 1901 to 1919.

pointment was to take place in the house of the king's sister. I
entered, my eyes lowered, and kissed the Shah's hand. Without
a word, he lifted my veil and examined my face, especially my
ears and neck. He recognized pretty girls by their earlobes! I
pleased him . . . and he declared that from that day on I would
belong to him. 'Have her wait for my return from the hunt!'
But unfortunately, most unfortunately, it was to be his last
hunt! He was assassinated in Kalagosh. And I never was one of
the 'king's two hundred women.'"

A good part of my adolescent rebellion was crystallized around
that cage containing all the summer's dust. I, a human being,
had to see the world from behind a meshwork veil, like a
prison, reminiscent of a partridge covered with its hood! It
appalled me and I didn't miss any opportunity to say so, but
we couldn't afford to violate tradition.

I was fourteen when my father died. At sixteen they married me off to a first cousin and I came to live in Kabul in the
house of my uncle and father-in-law, who was then a minister
at the court.

The evening before Djashen[5] in 1959—I was eighteen then
and already had two sons—Prince Daoud, who was prime
minister and the king's cousin, decided to have both his and his
brother's wife go out without a chador, asking that the ministers follow his example. My father-in-law couldn't wait for
the next day to tell me the good news. He woke me up in the
middle of the night: "You can finally walk around like a human
being!" he announced, his eyes shining with pleasure.

I was up at dawn, putting on my chador one last time to go
to the bazaar and buy some fabric. That day I cut and sewed—
frantically!—two coats that came down to the ankle, one for

---

[5]The national holiday, Independence Day, August 18.

my sister-in-law, and the other for myself. It was full summer, but we couldn't shock the mullahs! We put on very dark
sunglasses and scarves to cover up our hair. And in this getup
we went to the party with my husband. My mother-in-law was
annoyed, and her youngest son left, outraged and slamming
the door—he couldn't say anything since the head of the family
had given his permission.

In the tent reserved for the women of the royal family, our
entrance did not go unnoticed: I, the daughter of a Pashtun
mountain lord, was among the first to have dared the impossible. I was more than a little proud!

Gradually, for celebrations, ministers were invited with
their wives, as were governors and army officers. Letters were
sent to the secondary schools, to hospitals, every sector of the
administration, and to the Women's Association.

Two years later a law on the veil came out, ordering all
women in the public sector, schoolgirls, and students, to dress
Western style. But it was years before it was fully implemented.

In Kandahar, there were movements opposing this first
women's liberation. True battles between extremists and the
army that had come as reinforcement for the capital city. Several years later, some fanatics assaulted women by shooting
them in the legs or throwing acid in their faces. Then bit by bit
everything calmed down. Girls who have been to secondary
school refuse to wear the chador after their marriage.[6]

When the upper-class women abandoned the chador,
working-class women adopted it. Rural women work side by
side with the men, their faces bare; they wear a veil over their
hair just as the men wear a cap or turban. Hazara women, who

---

[6]In 1978, in Kabul, women and young girls generally wore Western
clothes, with stockings, a lightweight white or colored scarf, and long
sleeves.

did not use to wear the chador when they came from the village, do not leave their homes unveiled, afraid of what people will say.

When it comes to this, it often is just as much the women as the men who enforce a custom. They go in circles in a closed environment that sometimes encourages pettiness or bitterness: women will speak maliciously of women because they have no other interest, no other points of reference than the world in which they are confined, and, by force of circumstance, they endorse their own alienation. Society is made for men and they know it. First it is the mother who will raise her son as a superior being and in her daughter will unconsciously inculcate the disdain she has for herself. In the same context, the hardness, not to say cruelty, of some mothers-in-law can be explained: a woman, as insignificant as she is herself, is coming to frustrate the only relationship she has been able to have with someone from the master caste: her son, who of her children was the one worth bringing into the world.

Between a rural woman and myself there is one basic difference: I know my rights, whereas she thinks she doesn't have any.

Her life is much harder than mine, also. In the morning, she is running around the mountain looking for wood. Comes back down. In a haze of fatigue she feeds the animals, milks them, goes to work in the fields with her husband, bakes the bread at home in the tandour, and takes care of the cows and the sheep. Turkoman women wear their eyes out day and night as they weave. In Nuristan, they would yoke women to the animals to terrace the fields on the slopes and guide the animals to keep them from falling! But not one of these women has ever gotten perturbed: their lives are laid out for them and they have no way of changing things; no more than they can question their destiny. It is our task to make them into conscious human beings.

I didn't have the luck of having any daughters, but in rais-
ing my three sons I have tried to counterbalance the influence
of the social environment. I've accustomed them to mending
a piece of clothing themselves, to doing their laundry, and to
helping with household chores, rather rare events in Afghanistan, where such tasks, reserved exclusively for women, are
humiliating for boys.[7] I keep telling them that when they get
married it will be to a woman who is their equal, who'll work
outside of the house like them and with whom they'll have
to share the tasks at home. That only with such a balance will
both they and their wives be happy.

This education should start from their earliest childhood on,
for boys as well as girls. As long as mothers have contempt for
women, their daughters will underestimate themselves throughout their lives; it is a feeling etched inside their head since birth:
women are less strong, less intelligent, and more fearful. They
should be pretty, enchanting as a flower; they were meant to be
perfumed and admired, to gratify and delight men.

In Persian literature, her body is white and soft as silk; she is a
star, a gazelle, a doe, or a narcissus; her figure is a cypress and her
breasts two pomegranates. The silvery light of her cheeks resembles
the moon; her curls are made of ebony, jade, musk, or amber. Her
teeth are pearls of the beautiful sea; her lips are honey, chalcedony,
or ruby. Woman exists solely in relation to man: her whole life
is devoted to the well-being of others, and she must fashion her
personality to suit the taste of man. How could she possibly begin
to understand that she is as worthy as he?

In contrast to the women of the era of the Prophet, today

---

[7]When I told Shirîn that I would have liked my own brothers to have
been raised like her sons, she burst out laughing and said that women
across the world had plenty of work to do.

we are able to work to earn a living for ourselves and our children; we no longer need to depend on men, like objects—a teapot, two teapots, four teapots; one glass, two glasses, four glasses at the man's disposal.

Obviously, women have as many natural gifts as men. Those women who are lucky enough to obtain an education are proving that in many areas they can be superior to men, for their life experience is often richer and more profound than that of their companions, convinced of their virile strength and rather unconcerned with testing it.

Thanks to the education my father gave me, I've never suffered from any inferiority complex in comparison to men: I am a human being, as capable of thinking and acting as they are.

Three months after putting my chador away, I started working. I had to make money because my husband was doing his military service and then, too, I was passionate about my work. In the high school where I taught, the battle against the chador was making waves: the girls were having a lot of trouble convincing their fathers to let them go to school with their faces uncovered—black uniform, black stockings, little white veil. I kept telling the students that the teachings of the Koran should not be confused with barbaric customs. I kept trying to give them the courage to face up to a father who was threatening to lock them in the house. "If you have the strength of will," I used to say to them, "the law is with you and nobody can prevent you from following it." I've always fought this way, knowing full well that as long as women are not educated they won't want to and therefore cannot develop; thus, it is by the will of women alone that progress can be made.

When educational broadcasts for women were being produced at Radio-Kabul, I enthusiastically threw myself into the new work that was offered me. I had to prepare lectures

in Pashtun and Dari,[8] directed at women to familiarize them
with the existing laws in their favor, the rights they did not
know about. It was an entirely new experiment. Sometimes
they would phone at the last minute asking me to prepare a
talk about women, their rights within Islam and in the laws
of our country. They would ask me to read poems in honor of
women. That really excited me.

Why such a slow evolution when you think of the work we
and the women's associations did? I think that women's liberation goes hand in hand with a country's general progress. And
one cannot speak of development when most of the population, both male and female, is illiterate. Women's emancipation
works only with the democratization of a country, which was
hardly what the governing power before the arrival of the Communists wanted to have.

Yet, during difficult periods I have been known to be
envious of the illiterate farm woman. She doesn't dwell on her
misery and endures her life without rebelling, and so she seems
happier than we, for we are conscious of our possibilities and
are suffering every minute from the shackles men impose on
us. They themselves are often profoundly similar to their rural
peers. When horizons open up for the educated woman, the
Afghan male is not ready to forgo his privileges as absolute
master.

I have frequently met men who are remarkably cultured and
intelligent, capable of the most feminist of discussions, who
then reveal themselves to be veritable little tyrants at home,
pure products of the environment. This can be easily explained.
Girls and boys are separated by a barrier of prohibitions. They
are turned in two diametrically opposed directions, girls toward
the interior, boys toward the exterior.

---

[8]The Persian spoken in Afghanistan.

The shadow or the very reflection of women is absent from the world of men: they don't speak about a sister, a mother, or a wife; that would show a lack of respect in front of a brother, a son, or a husband. In the end, then, when does the moment come when respect changes to disdain or indifference? For many men, women are no more than just another household object.

For a rural woman, the urban woman is the lucky one: she doesn't work like a beast, she has a comfortable house . . . Country women complain about material poverty, the loads that break their backs, the fire of the tandour that burns their eyes, and of their hands and feet cracked from the cold. The awareness of their destitution lies in their creaking bones and their aching bodies; it is not in their head, but it comes down to the same thing. One day one of them said to me: "May it please God, if we could go back, may he make me a stone rather than a woman!"

I am privileged, and yet I can't remember any period in my life that I was calm and serene. When I was small, I hurt because I didn't have a mother; then my father, the only human being who loved me, died; and finally, I was married too young.

I have always felt the need for self-affirmation—I had to prove to myself and to others that I was a human being worthy of respect, in my work, in the family, and to my husband. My life has been a war against everything that was out to diminish me.

In this battle, a few trips abroad have allowed me to situate myself as a woman from Afghanistan.

I have been to the United States and to Europe twice, societies where women seemed to have all the advantages and liberties of men. So many privileges compared to us! But as I thought about it more deeply, the benefits became blurred and I sensed a terrible void. What is there to be envied in a society where everything is slackened and sloppy? The prime objective there for everyone is material comfort. With commercials, television, an incessant conditioning of man, woman, and child, everything forces them to want nothing but their own material gratification. Over there everything seems based on money, possessions, social success, bigger salaries, because needs can only increase for people who are frustrated by thinking that they could have still more. Couples split up, children leave their parents and forget them; each person for himself and you have a dislocated society, made up of individuals who no longer know how to live together. It's absurd. There is no place anymore for what I hold dear: the achievement of man and woman, the grandeur that the human being cannot find in things but to which he can aspire in a spiritual quest by detaching himself specifically from these material conditions.

I don't deny that we must fight against the poverty of Afghanistan. Those who have had power in our country weren't true Muslims and were only thinking of their own gain. That is why we are living in a very unjust society. But what matters first of all, even for the poor, and what gives their lives meaning, is their faith in God, in the commandments of the religion that ought to make us into self-respecting men and women.

I love the family tradition here that obliges us to help and support one another. This tradition confers a sacred value upon the home and allows the laws of hospitality to always remain alive: we don't close in upon ourselves; we are always members of a community. Old men have their place in it as head of the family and aren't isolated as if they were no longer useful. They are respected, they are handled with care, for wisdom comes from them; they know, because they have lived, and the most sensible advice is expected to come from them. In the Pashtun tribes, important political decisions are made by the council of elderly men who meet and deliberate. If women have not openly had access to politics, the history of Afghanistan shows us examples of great kings, such as Ahmed Shah Baba, who used to consult their mothers before making choices that were supposed to direct the country's future. It happens that, when there are conflicts between tribes because of the flight of a girl or a woman, they send the oldest woman of the house to mediate with the offended party and beg their pardon. Out of regard for the respect owed the elderly, it would be quite irreverent to refuse negotiation.

I like the teaching of the Koran that encourages both man and woman to be pure and to be masters of their own bodies; the commandments concerning sexuality seem fair to me, for a certain purity of body and heart is essential to our fulfillment. It is the honor of the Afghan woman, and that has nothing to do with the subjugation in which she is held.

I believe deeply in Islam and I know that as Muslim women we have to fight to obtain what the Prophet required from men: they must recognize that men and women, equal before God, are both human beings. I demand the rights that are due us, and it seems to me that these are rights that men and women the world over have not yet obtained, not in communist regimes nor in capitalist countries. Finally, I think that a Muslim society is worthy of that name only to the extent that it is ready to submerge itself, humbly and generously, into the very heart of the texts on which it is based.

Reduced to silence in front of men more than in other ethnic groups, they say, Pashtun women practice a most original form of poetic expression among themselves. For example, they are the authors of the *landay,* the short regular poem in two lines, nine and thirteen syllables, which young girls and women sing as they go to fetch water by the river or when they dance during a celebration. They don't expect these songs to be heard, and often their echo gets lost in the mountains; their virtue is that of a liberating breath. They are cries from the heart: cries of distress, revolt, or provocation faced with a world that forbids them to love; sometimes cries of war to entreat men to defend the threatened heritage.

Our friend, the philosopher-poet Sayd Bahodine Majrouh,[9] who was assassinated in Peshawar in 1987, had—with his sister-in-law—collected some of these poems, which we translated together, with great concern for adhering as closely as possible to their expression in Pashtun.

In a society based on family, where marriages never take feelings into account, love is almost always a scandal. The woman is subjected to the greatest constraint: the man can travel or try his luck with another woman, but all that remains for the young girl is forced marriage to a *mouzigaï,* the "little horror" chosen by her parents.

They sing of the dreadful marriage they did not want and celebrate the imaginary Lover adorned with every virtue:

> *My father's house is a royal throne;*
> *Cursed be my father-in-law who makes me fall from this throne.*

> *I am ready to sacrifice myself for my brother;*
> *The little horror has his own sister, let her sacrifice herself for him!*

> *Cruel people, you see how an old man leads me to his bed*
> *And you ask why I weep and tear out my hair.*

> *One is dying from the desire of seeing me without delay;*
> *The other throws me to the foot of the bed and says that he is sleepy.*

> *Oh, my God! here is the night again,*
> *My body lies trembling in my bed.*

---

[9] *Ego Monstre,* vol. 1: *Le Voyageur de Minuit* [Midnight Voyager]; vol 2: *Le Rire des Amants* [Lovers' Laughter] (Paris: Phébus, 2002).

They sing of the pain of love:

You covered yourself with your shawl and sleep.
Your heart is not troubled by the burn marks of love.

I used to be more beautiful than a rose.
Inside your love I have grown yellow like the orange.

I did not know suffering before;
That is why I was growing straight as a pine tree.

On the final day, God will know all too well
That it is because of you I will have died.

They bemoan separation:

The one who separated me from you has claws
From which I try to free myself, leaving shreds of flesh behind.

There's no hope left for recovery,
Separation's dragon has gnawed away at my heart.

Love is a precious stone, separation a dragon.
Whoever desires the stone will certainly be eaten by the dragon.

Separation arrived and the road branched off.
Death I accept, but not so separation.

They call for death:

May God give me death in my youth,
May my mother weep and my lover feel remorse!

On the final day, loudly I'll cry out
That I've come from this world, torn apart by anguish.

They hope for the impossible escape:

Sleep and reverie delight me
For only there can I encounter my love.

Light of my eyes and balm of my heart,
Oh, misery of love! I conceal you as I laugh.

Are you not ashamed, you with your white beard?
You caress my black hair and deep inside myself I laugh.

They praise their closeness to nature:

Oh God, make me a prairie flower,
Let the air that comes from my lover make me shiver!

My lover in a distant land,
Send me the seeds of reunion, so that I can make it grow.

May God transform you into a river flower,
So that I can inhale you when I fetch the water!

My friend is enraged with me.
To appease him, I would make the counsel of the wise descend
    from the stars.

Oh moon! please rise and illuminate the world
For my love is traveling in the heart of the mountains.

Oh, moon! stop your shining,
And don't betray my lover who is hugging the wall!

Spring is here and the pomegranate blooms.
For my absent lover, I shall save the pomegranates of my breasts
    from my garden.

They secretly nurture enticement:

My love, come running to me!
The little horror sleeps and you can kiss me now.

Come and look at me, don't be deprived of that pleasure!
No one will cut your throat over a simple look.

Change yourself into a Malang[10] *and come to me.*
No one has ever blocked the Malangs' way.

I shall reduce you to ashes
If I turn my gaze on you for just one moment!

May God cause you to be in love as I am,
So that I can see you walking through the streets like one who's lost.

Kiss me beneath my chin,
For my mother-in-law sees my face's every particle.

Gladly do I offer you my mouth.
Why are you stirring my vessels? I am all wet.

My love, come and kiss me quickly!
In a dream I saw you dead and I went mad.

Gently place your hand inside my wide sleeves
The pomegranates[11] from Kandahar have bloomed and ripened.

They proclaim their impatience:

Unhappy lover! Why did you not come?
Standing on the roof alone I waited all night long!

---

[10] A wandering hermit or "God's madman."
[11] A woman's breasts.

Already the fires of dawn are lit.
I am still sitting here, trying to make my sulky lover smile again!

If you want to go, then go!
Don't keep repeating constantly that you are leaving now.

They shout their contempt for weakness:

There I lie, ready to welcome him,
And my lover is shaking with fear that the little horror will
*   wake up!*

My lover is a pumpkin flower.
He is worthless and I'll throw him on the dung pile!

They sing of their faithfulness and courage:

My grief is not a garment that wears out.
As long as I shall live, I shall keep it on my body.

Only the beloved will have a seat on my chest.
It is not a public hall where meetings can be held.

Tomorrow morning I shall be killed because of you.
Don't go and say that you did not really love me!

I am in love, I am not a renegade.
They can cut off my beauty mark with a penknife!

In the final analysis, the woman always belongs to a "house." She doesn't leave her father's house until she is to become an integral part of someone else's. This place, whose pillar she is, and these lands that she has worked as much as any man are dear to her: this sacred possession is her homeland, her only reference point onto the world; if it is threatened, so is she.

The existence of the men and women of Afghanistan is sketched out against a common backdrop: home, territory, tribe, and the code of honor that directs them. A man's honor is linked to the dignity of all those to whom he is connected by family ties or marriage. He who insults one member of this community insults every member of it, for when a single person is under attack the whole group is threatened.

For such questions of honor, the most merciless judge of man is without any doubt his wife: man is the absolute master at home only if he has the respect of others and thereby proves capable of protecting his house. Between the Pashtun man and woman this is a kind of pact, a pact that is preserved only if the man defends the family's patrimony at the price of his own life. A Pashtun proverb states that the ram—hence the male—is made to have his throat cut as a sacrifice.

Some landays remind men of their duties as warriors:

Liberty is a young bride
For whom young men are ready to give up their life.

Liberty says: "I am a beloved woman;
Those who are slaves I shall not kiss!"

Fight so as to be a conqueror.
He who does not conquer must die!

You did not lose your life in battle.
Did God bring you back so that you can live as a coward?

My lover fled from the battle.
Would that I had kept for myself the kiss I gave him yesterday!

My lock of hair my mourning cloth, too bad!
I like that better than to see you vanquished.

Why would our young men not take out their rifles?
Did they not drink an Afghan woman's milk!

In the struggle for freedom, go and lose your life!
Angels will be the ones to carry your corpse away.[12]

Offer yourself wholly to liberty,
Each morning young girls will go and visit your grave.

My love was killed for the motherland.
I shall weave him a shroud of the threads of my hair.

May God make you a martyr on the tribe's forehead!
With your blood I shall draw a dot in the dimple of my chin.

In the foundation myth of the Afghan nation, it was with a landay that a young seventeen-year-old nomad girl, Malalaï, came to
renew the courage of the Afghan warriors who faced British troops
near the village of Maywand in 1880:[13]

If you do not die at Maywand, oh my beloved,
You will be a coward. May God protect you from this!

---

[12]In the popular mind, angels are female.
[13]The girls' lycée in Kabul, where French women taught, was called the Lycée
Malalaï.

Afghan Women Today

Having forgotten Afghanistan at the time of the collapse that followed the departure of the Soviets and the Communists, the world press once again began to cover Afghanistan when the Taliban attacked a historic legacy of humanity—the Buddhas of Bamiyan.

The West then turned its eyes toward the martyred country that had been torn apart and destroyed by twenty-three years of warfare. Of interest were the Taliban regime, public punishment (floggings, stonings, hangings), and the furious determination with which women were made to disappear beneath the chador. All of these were decisions, decrees, and laws coming under an ideology that is incomprehensible to those of us who believe that progress is vital to every human society.

Ninety-eight percent of Afghan men and women living in their country know nothing about the world: their village and its history are the only reference point by which they judge what is the right thing to do or think. Morals and customs come from the depth of the ages, repeated word for word from generation to generation.

Shirîn, my women friends from Kabul, and we Western women abhor the chador because, apart from the discomfort it imposes, it symbolizes women's oppression.

The chador was willingly adopted, as a form of coquetry, by some women of the working class in Kabul in the 1960s. Today, women are forced to wear the full veil with its small mesh-covered opening for the eyes and are obliged to stay locked up at home for fear of reprisals, when they could be working as teachers educating children in the schools, as civil servants helping their country with its reconstruction, and as doctors and nurses taking care of the entire population.

I have always been concerned to understand this society that, in many respects, has been able to uphold values that have disappeared from our world of liberalism and the race for consumerism in all its forms.

In Afghanistan, people die and are as capable of suffering as anywhere else, but their time is not the same as ours, and neither is duration. Distances are still calculated based on the number of hours it takes to reach a place.

For these reasons I am deeply convinced that many women in the rural areas today are living in the same way that Begom used to live in Nuristan or Nour Khânom in Hazarajad. These accounts, which I collected more than twenty years ago, continue to be a reliable source of information by which to understand how Afghan society functions.

Kabul is in ruins, but its people are forced to survive.

When invited to dinner by Afghan friends who live near Paris, I watched the video they had just received from Kabul—the celebration of a family wedding that took place in the spring of 2001.

The images moved us deeply: the ceremony (filming a wedding even inside the home is already defying a prohibition), the demeanor of this or that person, the wedding buffet; the women sitting on embroidered cushions and getting up one at a time for a few dance steps to the sound of tambourines. The men, forced to wear their beards cut to a length specified by Taliban law,[1] have their turn at dancing. I am seeing the wedding of Sultân and Nasrîn again, twenty years earlier. Identical dress, gestures, rituals, and behavior. The bride, beneath her veils and jewelry, shows a sad mask of

_____

[1] The believer must be able to grasp his beard with ease for the ritual of prayer.

propriety. But it cannot be denied that the atmosphere is not there. What has changed is the unhappiness you can read on people's faces, for you know very well that the family, reunited for a marriage on that day, suffers outside constraints that make life a little more difficult every morning for both men and women.

Putting forth certain Islamic laws that they have reinterpreted to their own ends, the Taliban wanted to purify the cities first of communist and then of Western influences, but they also claimed to be bringing order and justice to the countryside, where people were living under ancestral laws.

The agronomist Alain de Bures, who has been living and working in Afghanistan for twenty years, knows the country well. He wrote the following from Jalalabad in March 2001.

Let's talk about the education of girls. No more girls in school! The NGOs and other associations, thinking in the short term only, put on the pressure. They stop funds for aid in education at the risk of causing boys to be even more ignorant and of gaining sexual equality this time. Like pestered crabs, the Taliban huddle in a corner and hold on tightly, not giving an inch; they might as well lose their legs and pincers. It should be noted that the world backs off and moves on to other things.

Under this indifference, someone realizes one day that some girls' schools begin to reappear, gradually coming out of hiding. Rural middle schools admit some of them more or less cautiously. Everybody knows it, nobody talks about it. This suits many people, and the daughters of the Taliban go there with their peers to learn that the earth is round. But then some callow "expat" walks in, newly arrived from Scandinavia or Central Patagonia, and "discovers" the pearl, the diamond. He proclaims it to be sensational and publishes the scoop, organizes a "tour" on the spot for other nitwits. The

very next day, the governor of the province, the judge, and
the head of the military security take their sisters or daughters out of the school and have the place closed down. The
process of reawakening has been interrupted. Of course, there
is a deafening outcry from the Scandinavians or Patagonians,
attacking huge turbans and dyed beards. "What's this?" some
minister asks, taking offense. "There were schools that adolescent girls attended and I didn't know! It's abhorrent! This
must be eradicated wherever it takes place!" The awakening
has been halted definitively, at least for the time being within
the minister's circles.

Animals have a reflex that makes them resist any coercion
with instinctive and obtuse dislike. Thus, a newborn lamb,
desperately looking for the teat its mother offers it, will never
latch on if the shepherd pushes it beneath her, and it will spit
it right out if it's put in its mouth by force. But if you scratch
the lamb's back with a finger and very gently point it in the
right direction with just a bit of pressure (imitating its mother's
muzzle when sniffing it), it will find the nipple right away. Pull
a horse toward you by the bridle while looking it in the eyes
and you will be hard pressed to make him come forward. But
take the bridle under the lower jaw and walk beside him and
all will go well. The same holds true for the civil servant of the
Taliban.

In the village, if a woman is miserable it is because her
husband is miserable. Often the men are as much to be pitied
as the women. If you prevent boys from going to school by
refusing financial aid because girls have no right to it, it leads
to sexual equality in the most dangerous kind of ignorance. If
Massoud did not make his wife wear the veil, he would have no
credibility whatsoever among the Afghans.

In certain ethnic groups, a man gains notoriety for stealing
another man's wife. The cuckold normally repudiates his wife,

and it all stops there. Otherwise he kills the seducer. This is
what happens among the Pashaï, the Gujur, and the Nuristani.
Obviously, these are not the sorts of things one talks about. But
one day you hear that a certain woman is no longer at home;
you don't know whether the husband is going to reclaim her or
not. Discussions take place, and quite frequently these sorts of
things occur without it necessarily causing any drama.

Women are far from mute inside their homes, and they
know how to speak up when it is a question of defending their
rights. A short introduction is called for to understand the
story that follows. Since the Communists lost power there is no
further rural exodus. Quite the contrary. Only rural people are
living more or less decently today. Before, when a family had
three sons, one would leave for the city, another might become
a soldier, and their standard of living was so far superior to that
of the homesteader who had remained on the land so that the
urban brothers would not claim their share of the farm. From
generation to generation, the land effectively became the property of those who stayed in the village to cultivate it. Today,
families retreat to the villages and cousins are asking for what
is theirs, claiming the land that used to be their grandfathers'.

In one family I know, the dying father had left his land to
two sons and a daughter. The latter, who was not married, received a dower. Normally, the daughter has the right to half of
what is a son's share. Babô lives on her share without too many
problems. She is an old lady living with her brother who had
stayed in the village. The oldest brother went to Kabul, where
he had become an important merchant. Then the bombings reduce his fortune to ashes. He comes back to seek refuge in the
village and lives there for a while. As time goes by, his children
grow up, and one fine day he needs money to marry off one of
his sons. He goes to his sister and tells her that he is taking her
land. Babô, herself quite a strong character, gets angry, raises

her strident voice, and, grabbing a stick, hits her brother on the nose. They fight and bystanders have to separate them.

The next day, the old woman puts on her finest chador and, without telling anyone, goes through the village all by herself, rents a horse and carriage, and heads straight for the governor, a Taliban, to make a scene. They tell her to go and see the judge. She lodges a complaint against her brother. The judge listens to her and sends his investigators out. Two days later, the brother is taken to the public square, beaten on the soles of his feet, forced to give back the cow he had taken and to reimburse the money for the one he had sold. The case was decided in her favor.

More than twenty years of war have only exacerbated the wretchedness in Afghanistan. In times of peace, conflicts between marriage partners, ill treatment inflicted on some women by a mother-in-law or a husband, would often be resolved through mediation by a family member; redress of an infidelity was sometimes simply a question of money.

De Bures, who created the Association for Aid in Agricultural Development in Afghanistan, wrote to me about a young girl who had fled Kabul with her family when the Taliban arrived and has since been living in Peshawar, a frontier city on the Pakistani side. In this context, the girl's story is unfortunately simple and almost commonplace (her real name is not used for reasons of security):

Engaged against her will at the age of fourteen to a young man whose family was related to the "leaders of the resistance," she believed that once she was in Pakistan and could take advantage of the absence of her fiancé's family's influence, she would be able to break the arrangement. Four years go by. They hardly think of the agreement anymore. "Zarmina" goes to the Lycée Esmat, run by a Hazara lady

and funded by some of the Afghans of the diaspora. She is
a brilliant student, first of her class in everything. But then
the opposition, said to have been reduced to a dispirited
defensive stand, raised its head again, now boosted by the
sanctions coming down on the Taliban.

This is when the fiancé reappears in Peshawar, determined
to make his rightful claims on the young girl, who is now eighteen. All hell breaks loose: verbal threats and intimidation; one
day the young girl is attacked, a bottle of vitriolic acid held up
to her eyes, and it looks as if they're going to throw it in her
face. Her shock is so great that it takes her several weeks to get
over it. Then the boy's parents come to discuss their slighted
honor; their conduct is truly disturbing. No more school for
Zarmina, no more outings into the city; she cloisters herself
and grows seriously depressed. Her world has been turned
upside down in a way! For in the end, where are the Taliban
in this story of an Afghan woman? The fiancé's family consists
of educated and rather affluent people, the sort who oppose
the Taliban, people who have no problem whatsoever obtaining passports and visas, whereas Zarmina, whose life is falling
apart, can always go and tell her bad luck to some consul: they
will not give her the European or American visa that would put
her beyond reach anytime soon.

Via one of her cousins whom I had met in Paris, I sent "Zarmina"
a letter in which I suggested she write down her story so that it could
be published in this book. She answered me in English and the letter
that follows needs no commentary (names have been changed):

> Dear Isabelle Delloye, hi.
> I want to write something about my life that you
> wanted from me.

While I was child I studied at school. During that period I was engeged with a boy by the name of Mahmoud.

When I became young he proposed me but I
reject him, but he insist me that I should accept him.
Acutally he was one of the person who was very near
to mujahedin, that's why I accepted. When that people
left Kabul we imgrayed to Pakistan. On that time I
was very happy that we were far from each other but
unfortunatly after two years he come to Pakistan. Now
I felt danger in Pakistan, becuse said to me that I will
kill you or something like this but belefe me I am not
happy with him.

I am ready to kill my self, but not ready for getting
marride.

I don't know what should I do. I thought a lot but
no effect.

Plese help me and show me the way that what
should I do.

I will be looking forward for your letter.

P.S. Sorry, madame. I know English, but not very will.
If I have mistake forgive me.

With lots of love,

Zarmina

I asked the cousin why the father, who now supports his daughter,
did not lodge a complaint with a Pakistani judge against the young
man. He answered that it was impossible since the aggressor was elu-
sive, continuously going back and forth across the border between
Pakistan and Afghanistan. Zarmina's father does not have the means
to even hope of getting his daughter out of this trap by sending her to
Europe or the United States. All I could do was express my helpless
empathy, trying to point out that the young man might just grow
weary of the predicament. I hardly believed this myself, for when

honor is at stake only bargaining over financial compensation can unblock the situation and allow the young girl's release.

When we speak of Afghanistan it is always to bemoan the ruin and misery of its people. Life goes on in spite of everything. A young man from near Jalalabad testifies to this in a report in May 2000 by Sonia Kronlund:

"My wife is my cousin on my mother's side. We took the sheep to pasture together when we were small. When I'd come home from the village school I used to teach her how to read. We loved each other and we got married. I was sixteen. My brothers helped me pay the dowry. That was eight years ago and we are still happy together."

"What do you expect from your wife?"

"She shouldn't start an argument with me. She should spend money wisely, respect my friends, and love me."

"And what is a good husband?"

"A good husband should not stay at home, but go out to work. If his wife's friends come to visit, he should welcome them and not get angry. He must send his children to school and feed them. If a husband hits his wife, he is not a good husband. When husband and wife have an argument, the air in the house becomes stifling and the children are sad. Life goes by quickly: we should be joyful. Afghans like to laugh, but the war has wiped the smiles off our faces. We like to make music for the birth of a child or at a wedding. We like to make jokes. If we invite friends the Taliban threaten to punish us."

In another room, an old woman raises her voice:

"We have nothing anymore for our children. When the war comes close we leave for Pakistan, then we come back here.

You're hot beneath the chador, you see nothing and nobody pays any attention to you.

"The world isn't hearing our cries and our pain. Foreign countries help the fighters but not the population. To bring peace to Afghanistan, all they need to do is forbid the importation of weapons. After that, they could bring in a government that would be acceptable to everyone. Convey these words to the world, or I'll rip up my shirt!"

I had recorded Shirîn's narrative, her "Pashtun woman's words," in October 1978, just before leaving Afghanistan. Wanting to know how she interprets the evolution of her country and what future she sees for Afghans today, I contacted her again in the United States, where she went into exile with her family thirteen years ago.

June 21, 2001

Dear Isabelle,

It took a long time for your letter to reach me. I am really happy that we have found each other again, and I hope your family and you are doing well. What are your daughters and your son doing now?

My family has grown. Today I have four grandchildren between sixteen and nine years old. Dear friend, as you know, I am a true Muslim from the bottom of my heart, but I do not agree with the Taliban regime, which is not Islamic but actually almost its direct opposite.

You ask me to tell you my story since I left my country. My God, how painful that is!

Listen: I left Kabul in 1978 with my youngest son, Atiq, who was barely seven years old. Why? Because at that time the Communist Party was in power and we were opponents. The Red Army had made its entry into

Afghanistan to allow the local Communists to stay in power. As you know, most of the population was against them, and since Afghans are not the kind of people to obey just any authority and since they hold their freedom and their religion dear above all else, we resisted; that is why I left Afghanistan. At Zalmaï's [her oldest son's] invitation, we went to France, then spent almost two years in Germany. After that we went to live in Pakistan, because Walid [her second son] was living there as one of the leaders of the resistance. I had the privilege of doing the cooking for his group. This went on for eight years during which I was happy to be able to participate, in my own way, in the battle of the holy war. When the Afghan people won out over the superpower, the Red Army withdrew. We did not want to take part in the struggle for power that followed; it was a civil war and the Afghans were killing each other off. Thanks to my nephew Fazal Akbar, who had connections at the United States Embassy, we started an immigration application file for the whole family, but at first only my husband and I were accepted. Oh, only God knows how hard it was for me to leave Walid, his wife, and their daughter, Sarah, whom I love more than my own life. That little one was with me day and night, but I really had to leave her with her parents. Fortunately, the American INS later helped me and I was able to have them come ten months later.

Indeed, settling here wasn't too difficult for me; as you know, I had worked at the United Nations Information Center in Kabul and had been in contact with Americans for more than fifteen years. I didn't feel disoriented among them, but I wasn't able to get the least bit in welfare benefits. I work outside the house and at home as well. And I am still not retired.

Family harmony is not bad, with some disagreement between mother and daughter from time to time about certain things. My relationship with my grandchildren is excellent; I love them enormously and they are very sweet. We try to hold on to our Afghan culture and our traditions, but I know that will change and that they are already halfway American.

Dear Isabelle, I miss my country so very much! And I often lament the misfortune of my people. Over the past six years, I lost one treasured brother, a sister, and recently the parents of my sister-in-law, whose funeral was only five days ago. I am so upset for her; she is in Peshawar with her brothers. They are married, have children, and undoubtedly will hardly have any time to take care of her. That makes me sad. May God help her and, with her, all the world's women.

I hope you've been able to read my handwriting. Give my regards to your husband. Love to you and your children.

Sincerely,

Shirîn Majrouh

I have met several young Afghan women who were living in the United States. At home they speak Persian. In any case, the parents speak Persian to their children, who very frequently answer in English. The children are generally quite well integrated into the system, and they do well academically. Moreover, they keep the sense of hospitality intact and those refined manners so characteristic of the Afghans.

This is also true for young Afghans living in France. Even if they were not born here, many of them have become French citizens. It is striking to note the ease with which they very quickly adapted to the culture. They are friends with French youth their own age, but they retain pride in their Afghan origins, which is carefully preserved by the parents.

Trina, a gynecologist and obstetrician who stayed in Kabul until 1991, left because the weight of the communist regime became unbearable. Today she lives in Lyon with her husband and her two children, a twenty-year-old daughter and a seventeen-year-old son. The forty-six-year-old physician had to take all her medical exams over again when she arrived and finally chose geriatrics: "I began my career by bringing human beings into the world. Now I accompany them as they depart for the other shore."

I met Trina in Kabul in 1978. I was pregnant with my third child and wondering whether I should go back to France for the delivery. We had never had any occasion to go to a hospital in Kabul for treatment; if there was a problem we would consult the young doctors who followed one another at the French Embassy in lieu of doing their military service. Kabul lies at a high altitude; there was no pollution, the climate was dry and very beneficial, and strict hygiene regarding water and fresh produce kept us all in good health.

They recommended that I consult Dr. Trina Kokcha, a young gynecologist and obstetrician whose competence seemed to meet with universal approval of the foreign women living in Kabul. The first time we met, I decided that my baby would be born in Afghanistan, a country to which we were growing more attached with every passing day. Trina exuded a goodness and serenity that were striking in such a young doctor and inspired my complete confidence in her.

It was not possible to have an ultrasound, but the tests were fine and my pregnancy went smoothly until April 27, 1978, the day of the communist coup d'état, which brought instability and concern about the future with it. I was a month away from my due date, and Trina assured me that, with weekly examinations, there would be nothing to worry about and that when the time came she would schedule the delivery to avoid being caught by the curfew.

I had my baby as she had planned it, under the best conditions. He was born around five in the afternoon at the Masturat Hospital, the women's hospital of Kabul, and the next morning at dawn my husband came to take us back home. My memories of those moments are marvelous.

Trina's Story

I left Afghanistan in 1991. I had obtained a passport and a visa to go to France, where part of my family had been living for many years already, to be examined medically. I was suffering from terrible headaches and needed to have a scan. I was supposed to be accompanied by my husband and, since there was no one to look after my children, I managed to get a visa for all four of us from the French Embassy, where I knew the chargé d'affaires quite well (I had taken care of his wife twice, in 1983 and 1991). At the time I was director of family planning in Afghanistan and supposed to go to New York, after my medical tests, to attend an international conference in my field. The Communists were still in power in Kabul. We locked our apartment door and arrived in France.

The situation in Afghanistan was very bad. We were the last ones in our family to leave the country. My husband was an engineer with the Highways Department; I loved my work and politics were of no interest to me. But in spite of my desire to have nothing to do with politics, it had become more and more difficult to live in Kabul and continue my duties as a doctor, no matter what. When you no longer have family you are very isolated in Afghanistan. With the children growing—my daughter was nine and my son six—I didn't dare let them go out anymore. We had teachers come to the house to teach them English, Persian, and math. Once we were in France, it became obvious that we couldn't go back to Kabul, where our children would have no future at all.

I had no plans. I didn't even know whether I would be able to practice my profession. Three days after our arrival, we went to see the principal of the elementary school, close to my sister's house where we were living. He assured us that there would be a place for the children, that it was their right to receive an education. And we stayed.

I was born in Kabul on October 1, 1945. My father was a military man and had resigned from the army over a question of honor. My mother was the niece of King Nader Shah, the father of King Zaher Shah, who now lives in Rome.

My father's family belongs to the Barekzaï clan, a very large family, often linked to the royal family by marriage and with a great many ministers and ambassadors among them.

So it was an arranged marriage between two families of similar rank. I am the oldest and have three sisters and two brothers. We spent our childhood in Kabul in the modern center where there were a few residential buildings. I went to school at the Lycée Malalaï, where the principal and several of the teachers were French. My father spoke perfect French, as did most of the members of the ruling classes in the Kabul of that period. However, he sent my brothers to the Lycée Habibia, an English-speaking school, while his daughters were attending a French-speaking school.

I went to school like any other little girl. I'm not under the impression that my childhood was very different from that of young Western girls. After school, we'd go biking and my brothers played soccer. There were no specific restrictions, and I remember it as a very happy time. My father had no special

rules either for my mother or for us. He was not jealous. Our
was a harmonious world to some extent, thanks to our relative
affluence, but most of all because of my father's personality. He
was a very liberal man; it was our mother who made all the decisions at home. Big celebrations took place within the family,
which was very large, one day at one aunt's house, the next day
at another's. We played with each other. In the summer we'd
go to Paghman, seventeen kilometers from Kabul, to get some
fresh air on the banks of the river, where we'd have gigantic
picnics.

My father loved talking about everything with his children,
history and current events. Like many Afghan soldiers, he had
studied in Turkey. Upon his return, he joined the Afghan army,
which he left over a quarrel with Daoud, the king's cousin, who
was then minister of defense and would become the first president of Afghanistan in 1973. Thereafter, he devoted himself to
the Persian poet Bedel and to the classical music of our country,
which is very close to the music of India. He often organized
concerts in our house, attended by the finest Afghan musicians.

When, after having obtained my bac,[2] I took the entrance
examinations for the university, my grades were such that I
was able to begin medical school right away. My parents, who
wanted me to become a physician, were thrilled. In the beginning, it didn't matter so much to me, I didn't feel the calling all
that much. After the first year at university, the premed year,
I ranked second out of four hundred students. About a quar-
ter of those enrolled were girls. In the amphitheater, during
classes, the girls were in the front rows and the boys sat behind
them. The dean of the science department then suggested that
I accept a scholarship to study math and physics in Germany,

---

[2] [The *baccalauréat:* the diploma from the lycée, acquired only after passing
many stringent exams, is required for entry into university—Trans.]

in Bonn. I was very pleased and announced the news to my
father, who flatly refused, however. "You should practice a profession that will give you independence. What will the study of
mathematics provide you with?" And so I started my first year
of medical school in Kabul. The first in our class was also a girl,
and, after three months, one of the anatomy professors nomi-
nated us for two scholarships in medicine in Poland. My father
immediately advised me to accept. I was seventeen and a half.
My father didn't hesitate for an instant, and neither did I.

I left without knowing a word of Polish. Once there, I
studied the language for seven months, and this allowed me to
finish my entire medical study in Warsaw, including my spe-
cialization in obstetrics and gynecology. I went back home in
1975. Eleven years of studying, very difficult in the beginning,
since I spoke no Polish and felt down in the dumps. But I had
a regular correspondence going with my family and the study
was all-absorbing. At first, during the year I was learning Polish, I was living with the other Afghan girl, and with a Greek
and a Lebanese girl, four to a room in the university residence.
Then my Afghan roommate went to study in another city—
she became a pediatrician. I was left with the Lebanese, Lena,
with whom I'm still in touch today, thanks to the perseverance
of that loyal friend who did everything to track me down after
I arrived in France.

Every other year I used to spend a month's summer vacation in Europe, visiting members of the family, and one month
in Kabul with my parents. I was very free and depended on
no one. There were no Afghans around me, and I was entirely
immersed in the international environment of the students in
Warsaw. I worked all the time, with the handicap of the language, which I didn't master until the end of the third year. But
I never had to repeat. My favorite pastime was bridge: I played
with my friends as soon as we had a moment off.

So time passed. Since the Poles detested the Russians, the study of medicine used European and American practices as their reference. The material was up-to-date, and the professors were competent.

Before returning to Afghanistan, I went to France to visit my sister who was studying there, but I was eager to go back to my country.

In Kabul, I began to work at Masturat, the university hospital for women. I was a beginning practitioner and had to take courses at the university in obstetrics and gynecology, my specialty. I had been trained to do every kind of gynecological surgery. In Poland, Professors Rszkowski and Zachwiej, who taught me in my last year there and knew I would be returning to my own country, had insisted on my learning everything that could possibly be done in surgery "for extreme cases in that mountainous land"! They were thinking, and rightly so, that I would have to manage on my own and be ready to face up to anything.

So I returned to Afghanistan when I was twenty-eight, prepared for all eventualities and confident in my knowledge. The hospital's gynecological team consisted of four men. All of them had many years of experience. They saw my arrival with some misgiving, because in contrast to them I had not been trained in either France or the United States. On my third day there, one of them invited me to attend his course at the medical school for fifth-year students. There were some one hundred students present. At the time, I didn't know the technical terminology in Persian. The professor told them: "Let me introduce a young doctor to you who has just arrived from Warsaw. Today, she will give the class in inflammations and cervical polyps." Without having told me anything in advance! Fortunately, I had taken the final exam in my specialty just two months earlier and fully mastered the subject. I kept my composure and took the floor: "I regret not having been alerted to the fact that I was to teach the class today. I have been working at Masturat for just three days after eleven years of studying abroad. I learned the terms in Latin and don't yet know their equivalents in Persian. Since the Latin terminology is very close to the French and the English, if you should not understand certain Latin words, you can always ask your professor, who will translate them for you." My class resembled a dialogue of doctors in Molière! In Poland, an initiation into Latin was required in the first year, and all diagnoses were written in Latin. On that day, I wasn't sorry. I taught the full class, which lasted for one and a half hours. And the professor knew that I had mastered my subject.

Three months later his wife and sisters-in-law had become my patients.

But at the hospital it took them a while to accept my authority as a physician in charge. It was only gradually that I gained their respect. Six months after my arrival, I was on duty, and the head of the department, Professor Anwari, who attended an operation I had to perform on a young woman journalist he knew, simply greeted me with a "You're good" and then left.

Every imaginable case of pathology would come through the department, and we had no equipment with which to do ultrasounds or scans. The X-ray machine worked only during the daytime. Laboratory analyses could be done during the day. We had a wooden fetuscope. During an examination, we had to make the diagnosis by palpitation: polyhydramnios, twin pregnancy, and so on, and emergency surgery could be done during the night.

Rural women would come to the hospital only if there was a serious problem. If the delivery was too difficult, their husbands in a panic would bring them in so that we would save

them from dying. I very often saw women coming in suffering
from a ruptured uterus, something that is very rare in France.
The child died, and the mother, in a state of shock, would be in
danger of septicemia.

I will always remember the first time I was on duty as well
as the woman who came in, having just climbed the stairs to
the second floor by herself. She was Pashtun from a village
close to the capital city. I could tell from an exterior examination of her belly that she had a ruptured uterus, that she was
fully dilated, and that the baby's head was stuck in the pelvis.
She should have been in a state of shock, yet her pressure was
normal. I couldn't believe my eyes or my ears, for she was
telling me about herself as if there were nothing wrong. It was
her seventh child and she was used to delivering at home, but
this time she knew something wasn't right and she had come
with her husband by taxi. Deliveries that follow each other too
closely give the organism no time to recuperate. The woman
lacks calcium and all the trace elements she needs for a smooth
pregnancy.

My colleagues watched me work, and I continued learning
the histopathology of gynecology, outside my hours on duty
and thanks to Professor Madjid Seraj, by reading slides and
examining biopsies and gynecological tumors.

There was a plan in the works to create a center for cobalt
therapy with international aid for the treatment of cancer.
Since I was very interested, I accepted going to Hungary for
training. This was in 1977. When the center was established
at the large Aliabad Hospital, in late 1977, I was responsible
for treating various forms of gynecological cancer. I went for
consultations there two half days a week. In addition, I did
consultations in gynecology, obstetrics, and family planning
on Tuesdays in the Moyna-Khané-Markazi Center in Kabul,
where care was provided free of charge. All the doctors at the

hospital were to donate part of their time to this center. We used to see people from both the country and the city there who had no money and who'd come almost as a last resort, for there was no law that forced anyone to declare a pregnancy or submit to prenatal examinations. Social welfare was not known in Afghanistan, but under King Zaher Shah and President Daoud all health care and most of the medications were free of charge in the public hospitals of Kabul. Only blood, in the case of surgery, had to be bought or provided on the spot by a family member.

My whole life was devoted to my work: courses at the medical school, being on duty at the hospital, the anticancer center, and the city's health center.

There were also many cases of sterility in Afghanistan, both male and female, and I became particularly interested in that problem.

I was becoming known. One day, a man who had asked to meet me, noticing my small stature and young age, called out: "That's you? The famous Doctor Trina, such a tiny little thing!"

Another time, I received a gentleman about sixty years old who had come from Jalalabad with his three wives. "Madame," he said to me, "I have three wives and no children and since I've heard that you are a fine doctor, we have come to see you." I told him to come to the Masturat Hospital the next day so that I could examine his wives and him as well. I added that he should bring some sperm for analysis.

I am sure that he had seen many other physicians before he came to me. The wives were in good health. The lab technician who had done the sperm analysis came in, saying: "There is not a single sperm here! The man is sterile." When I told the patient that his wives were very healthy but that the problem was his, he said to me in a fury: "Everybody is talking about

Doctor Trina here and Doctor Trina there, but you don't know anything, you're a nothing in the end!"

During one of my consultation sessions, a young soldier in uniform came in and said: "I was married three years ago, we have no children and the problem is mine. I've been examined and I am sterile, but my wife doesn't know it. I want to have a child and I'd like you to find me some sperm." I answered that it was up to him to bring the sperm, and when he asked I explained how we could proceed at the right moment in his wife's cycle. Two weeks later, he came with her and brought sperm. Nine months later, I saw them again when he came to ask me to examine his wife and tell her whether she could have the baby at home. She was in perfect health, but it was better to be delivered at the hospital, for we were under the communist regime and there was a curfew. But I didn't see them again. All of this happened in the most natural fashion and without wasting any words.

Another very nice story describes the mentality of the Afghans quite well, for they are not at all the backward people that the Taliban would have you believe.

This is about a couple from Djunobi, Pashtun people from the south of Afghanistan. The woman was very young and dressed in the heavy, brightly colored clothes of rural women; the man, in traditional costume, was about thirty. He was a truck driver between Pakistan and Afghanistan. They'd been married for three or four years and had no children. We examined them both, and this revealed that the husband was sterile. He had an immediate reaction of sadness, as did his wife, who was there with him. They were sitting close together, not touching, and then like a chorus they asked whether there was any solution. They hadn't exchanged a glance. I could tell they loved each other very much. She hardly spoke any Persian since her language was Pashtun. Six months later they came back to see me again, telling me that they had rented a house in Kabul and that the husband had found work as driver for the Ministry of Agriculture. They wanted to do something to have a child. I explained the procedure to be followed. If they could find a sperm donor, there were days in the woman's cycle when a simple procedure could be done, but it wasn't always successful. These were illiterate people. I gave the young woman a thermometer and explained to her how to recognize the right day for coming to the hospital (when the mercury goes beyond the red spot), and on that same day the husband was to bring in sperm. He told us that he had suggested to other drivers that he would buy sperm from them, claiming he would sell it to a laboratory. This is how they made it to the hospital with a small bottle of sperm under the arm to keep it at body temperature. In this way they had three children. They were very simple, very pure people, who understood the meaning of it all very well. When DjonMomad, the first son, was born, the woman was overjoyed. But remember that she spoke Pashtun, didn't know how to read or write, and when the child was one year old and about to say his first word, she confided to me what she was worried about: "My God, the little one's father is from Kabul and speaks only Persian! God protect us from the shame of this!" Of course, when the first word the child spoke turned out to be *moré* (*mama* in Pashtun), the young woman exclaimed, "Thank God, he has not dishonored us!"

She came back every month with her husband during each of her pregnancies for a checkup. He adored his children. She would bring me a live chicken as a present, hidden beneath her coat before coming into the hospital, and once she sat down she'd let it loose and it would fly around the room doing its business everywhere . . . In the end, the woman spoke Persian very well. We really liked each other very much. I wonder what's become of her today?

I used to see all sorts of people at my consultations, every case that a gynecologist, obstetrician, and cancer specialist can encounter. In Afghanistan, we are confronted with forms of pathology that are typical of very poor countries: tuberculosis often has disastrous results, causing pelvic tumors and sterility. But the private lives of men and women are in no way different from those of men and women who live in the societies where sexuality is presumably "liberated." Female homosexuality exists as well. The problems that couples have are the same: impotence, infidelity, dissatisfaction, sterility; and the capacity for love and tenderness is as great as in any happy couple anywhere else in the world.

I would see women of all classes, some of them very poor, others from the middle class, and then also wives of ministers and ambassadors posted in Kabul. Word of mouth worked very well.

In April 1978, it was a Thursday, I was operating. There was a lot of work that day and I hadn't had the opportunity to leave the O.R. before three o'clock in the afternoon. The communist coup d'état had taken place without my even knowing it. I thought there was a thunderstorm outside, that was all. I went home with the husband of one of my patients who was a taxi driver. The city was full of tanks, there was shooting everywhere, but we managed to get home without any problems.

I was on duty the next day and did my work as usual.

In 1980, I was continuing my consultations at the free health center until a Russian gynecologist claimed I was overshadowing her and preventing patients from seeing her. So I stopped going there, and nobody ever asked me why.

Then, after a period of time, the Russians decided to shut down the Masturat Hospital and to transfer the teaching hospital to a larger one. I was opposed to this move, convinced that health-care centers should in fact be increased in number. The

important physicians had all left the country. I was the only
one of my team with the young doctors to have stayed put.
They did close the hospital in the end, however.

I had some patients who were used to visiting me free of
charge at Masturat. When I started at the new hospital where I
expected to see my usual patients, the director criticized me for
holding "private consultations" and refused to admit that this
was a service to be rendered to the poor. When I came home,
I told the story to my parents; a cousin, who happened to be
there that day, suggested lending me one room in his apartment, right across the street from us. He ordered a nameplate
that said "Doctor Trina, gynecologist-obstetrician" in white on
a blue background. A young male friend of his, a law student,
offered his services as a pro bono secretary, and I began to receive patients in this improvised "office." After just one month
I had a practice.

It was July 1982. I was going to the hospital in the morning, taught courses at the university, and saw my patients in the
afternoon from four or five o'clock on. I didn't ask any questions about their husbands' profession, and often I found out
only by chance who they were. I've never been concerned about
politics, and I certainly didn't want to be brought up-to-date.
My job as a doctor came before everything else. And my patients were attached to me. Twice I did an emergency delivery
at the office. The woman had refused to go to the hospital, in
spite of my recommendations earlier that very morning. In the
evening, as I was leaving my practice, I found her there, sitting
and twisting and turning, ready to give birth. Yet, she was accompanied by her mother-in-law and several other women. It
was exactly the same scene both times.

At the time I was living in an apartment by myself in a
building that belonged to my father. The hospital salary was
laughable, and my parents were even giving me an allowance.

When I was paid after a delay of several months I reimbursed my father completely. That's only normal. I needed nothing and wasn't preoccupied with money questions since I had all the essentials.

My father died very suddenly after an illness, in 1982.

I had then been married for two years.

I was married in April 1980, as was done for a hundred years in Afghanistan. In my generation and my social class boys and girls choose each other freely.

I was the oldest of the children and one of my brothers had already married, while one of my sisters was engaged. Another sister had left the country with her husband for the United States.

My parents wanted to see me married. My sisters and my sister-in-law were trying to have me meet someone; the nurses, too, wanted to introduce me to this or that doctor. But I was absorbed in my work and found such joy in it that I could think of nothing else. I'd grab something for lunch without joining the others in the dining room for interns and specialists. I was like a horse in its furrow, its eyes protected by blinders.

The parents who asked me in marriage for their son had seen me for the first time on television where I was giving advice to pregnant women.

I was thirty-six years old, but my parents arranged everything. They were so insistent that I couldn't say no. That was enough for history to take its course. One day when I came home from the hospital, I found a few people at the house: it was my engagement party, which my future husband himself did not attend. We saw each other once thereafter for about ten minutes. The ceremony took place three months later. They declared us husband and wife, and we have remained so until today.

In September 1983, I had to have surgery for a tumor in

France, in Lyon, where my brother was living. I was able to
obtain a passport and the needed authorization thanks only to
one of my students who had become an important member of
the Party. My mother and my two-year-old daughter came with
me. My husband stayed in Kabul. When I arrived in France,
I was three months pregnant. The examinations I had to have
were dangerous for the baby, but I refused to have the pregnancy terminated and had to wait to finish the fifth month.
At that point I was operated on for the tumor, which was not
cancerous, fortunately. Three weeks later I went back to Kabul.
I wanted my son to be born in Kabul. My mother, who also
had health problems, stayed with my brother and never came
back to Afghanistan again.

My husband was at home, and I was still hoping that when
the Russians and the Communists left, the war would stop, and
that all would go back to normal. I had family in the United
States and in France. I could have emigrated, but I loved my
country deeply.

Since the gynecology and obstetrics department had been
moved to the Zâheshga Hospital, I had not felt comfortable
there; it was a much larger place with many more beds. On the
average there were about eighty deliveries a day and sometimes
as many as one hundred and forty.[3] Mattresses everywhere,
including the hallways. Women would stay in the hospital
for a maximum of four or five hours and then they'd be sent
home. There were Russian counselors and nurses, and many
members of the Afghan Party; it was a factory where politics
played a greater role than medicine. As for me, I went there

---

[3]In 1987, there were 29,523 deliveries in the Zâheshga Hospital, 6,254
gynecological surgical operations, 437 of those being serious cases. Trina
adds: "What has become of the 35,340 patients since the Taliban closed
this establishment, the only maternity hospital in Kabul?"

every morning, operated, gave my courses, and participated in
the medical meetings with the interns. But I feared the lack of
care I was observing everywhere. Hygiene was deplorable. The
patients had to buy all their medications. The health system
had deteriorated in an unbelievable way. During a very delicate operation, in 1983, a Russian nurse who was assisting me
handed me the wrong instrument. I rarely get upset, but that
day I demanded that the woman be replaced by an Afghan
nurse. I said that I would stop the operation until this one
had left the O.R. And that is what she did, she had to. So, I
had caused myself to be noticed on several occasions, showing
clearly that the only thing that mattered to me was medicine
and I wouldn't take part in any political meetings. A young
Afghan woman, freshly arrived from the Soviet Union, had become the hospital's vice president. Bureaucracy was paralyzing
everything. If I came late from my courses to clock in for duty,
they saw it as my having been altogether absent. In 1984, that
happened eleven times in a row. Eleven times I had to write
a letter of explanation to state that I was present since I had
been teaching. According to the law, three days of unjustified
absence were enough to be let go. Obviously, it was one way of
trying to discourage me, of punishing me for not participating
in the political life. So then I went to the ministry to apply for
a leave without pay. No question of being laid off. I stopped
working at the hospital and teaching courses to the medical
school interns and devoted myself to my private practice and
my children. I took notes on every medical case that came my
way in order to do research with a view to publishing material
on the pathology typical of Afghanistan. I had, for example,
complete files on male sterility. This lasted until 1987.

At that point, the communist government decided to
implement a policy of national reconciliation, asking those
who had remained aloof from the Party to take up their posi-

tions once again. I was called several times by the Minister of
Health; they would like me to pick up my work again at the
hospital as well as at the health center, which I refused to do on
three different occasions.

One evening around eight o'clock, as my husband and I
were watching television, the telephone rang. It was one of my
patients, the wife of Nadjib, the president of Afghanistan! "My
husband would like to speak with you," she said. "Right now."
They sent a car for me and the president received me, saying:
"Doctor Trina, tomorrow you will take over the directorship of
Zâheshga Hospital. You will be introduced to the departments
tomorrow morning." I tried to offer the objection that if I
was able to practice my profession as a medical doctor, I was
completely ignorant of anything administrative. "Everything
has been taken care of. You should be at there at ten o'clock,
and I am counting on you to cooperate with the Ministry:
the Afghan women need you! All the power is in your hands,
nobody will oppose you. It is up to you to go ahead with any
reforms." There was nothing to do but to accept. The following day, in the presence of the minister, the vice minister, and
all the directors, I was named president and head of all sections,
which included more than four hundred employees, many of
whom were Party members. This was the same hospital where
four years earlier they had gently pushed me out.

That same day, I alerted the leader of the Party sector of
the hospital that our tasks would be totally dissimilar. I as-
sembled the Afghan personnel members who were competent
in obstetrics and gynecology to encourage them to count as
much as possible on their own strengths and to avoid consulting the Russian advisers. They all knew me. Then I brought
the Russians together, telling them that we would call on them
only when needed. From that day onward, not a single Russian operated at Zâheshga Hospital. They left a few months

later. Nadjib had not lied: he really gave me the power to take
the hospital in hand again. But in order to do that I had been
forced to obey an order.

My official function was taking up all my time and I was
being pressured, rather blatantly, about the activities of my
private practice: they wanted to know whom I saw and, indeed,
have me give them information about whom I saw—something
I obviously always refused to do. For the ten months that I
held the position I had been assigned at Zâheshga Hospital, I
stopped seeing patients privately.

I wasn't very comfortable there: the statue of Lenin at the
front entrance of the hospital seemed to be taunting me. I was
constantly surrounded by Party members. Yes, that went on for
ten months. Until I picked up contact with the Association of
Family Planning of Afghanistan, a nongovernmental organization, aided by the International Planned Parenthood Federa-
tion (IPPF), whose headquarters are in London. This group,
with sixty-four clinics in every city in Afghanistan, needed a director in Kabul. I sent in my application and was soon elected
to be the executive director of Family Planning of Afghanistan.
I immediately handed in my resignation from the hospital,
and I think they must have been pleased to be rid of me. They
replaced me with a doctor who was a Party member.

The IPPF had divided the globe into six sections. Afghanistan, as a Muslim country, was part of the zone connected to
the Arab world. The center of this area was Tunis. So, at the
time, I was taking frequent trips to the North African nations
to defend budgets and present plans for popular education. We
created accelerated training programs for rural midwives. We
used to pay these women to come and do a week's training in
Kabul. They would then go home with a small suitcase full of
medications and dressings, but God knows if they were able to
do anything at all: there was war in the villages.

We had also started up a mobile unit that went around safe regions. I was not working for the government, since the association was independent. My one obsession was to stay in Afghanistan.

I held that position for three years.

In 1989, I reopened my office at the request of my patients. Although I was passionate about my work, I found the situation more and more arduous. My husband had been removed as engineer working with the Soviets in charge of the Ministry of Public Works for reasons of "noncooperation." Since I was supposed to attend a Family Planning meeting in New York and I had started getting my migraines again, I applied for a passport and a visa for France for myself as well for my husband and children. The authorities knew I wouldn't return, and yet they approved my request without any difficulty.

We arrived in France, where we immediately applied for asylum. I sent a telegram to New York to let them know that I wouldn't be attending the meeting. We decided to stay in Lyon, for the children, hoping to go back to Kabul when the war ended.

But the civil war continued with renewed vigor after the Communists departed. And we are still here.

My husband didn't speak a word of French, nor did my children. But the little ones adapted very quickly, not even losing one year in their schooling. After three months they were speaking like every other little French child their age. Ten months after applying for political asylum, we were accepted.

I wanted to work and knew that my diplomas would not be recognized in France. While redoing the entire cycle of medical studies in order to be able to practice, I also had to earn a living for the children and myself. I tried to be a nanny but was told that I didn't have the proper training! I wanted to be a nurse but had to do the last three months of nursing school. I would have done that had I not needed to take another exam at the very same time to obtain medical equivalency. Finally, I found a job "serving as an intern" at the hospital. Many foreign physicians are employed this way, without their diploma or their qualifications as a practitioner being recognized for all that.

I sent letters to every department of gynecology in the region, but they had no work for me. The only interesting opportunities were more than a hundred kilometers away. I didn't want the children to have to change schools and surroundings for fear that they would lose ground. Here they had their friends, their cousins, and stability.

In 1995, I took the equivalency exam in general medicine. The written portion was given in February in Lyon, the oral seven months later in Paris. After having practiced obstetrics and gynecology for twenty years, I had to do every part of general medicine again. Fortunately, I passed on the first try. I think I was lucky. But permission to practice my profession did not come for another three years.

By the time I became board certified, it was 1998. The vice president announced that I would not be able to perform any surgery in France other than cesarean sections because I didn't have the surgeon's diploma. I had the right to open an office, but one needed a great deal of money to do that. With my medical assistant's salary and at my age, how could I borrow enough capital for such a thing?

At the time, I was working in a geriatric department, and I loved my patients and the general medicine I practiced there. Then I was hired as temporary employee at the Hôtel-Dieu, the main hospital, where I have been practicing as a gynecologist ever since.

When the center for cobalt therapy was opened in Kabul in 1977, the word *palliative* was used a great deal, for the patients that came to us were frequently in the terminal stage of the

cancer they had. In many cases, their condition called for a
palliative or analgesic radiotherapy. There was no morphine,
and quite often we would have to ask the anesthesiologists for
leftover vials of Dolosal that we would use to quiet the pain
of terminal patients.

In Lyon, thanks to one of the pioneers of palliative care,
Madame Filbert, a marvelous woman, I began that work and
ended up by getting a diploma in this specialty. Presently, I am
in charge of a palliative care unit at the hospital of the Hospices
Civils in Lyon.

That is my story. I've been caught in a series of traps that
frequently prevented me from making the choices I wanted to
make. You can call it destiny if you want. In any case, one thing
makes me proud: my children have done well in school and
have the kind of life children their age should have.

I want them to find their way. I love France, but I wish
with all my heart that one day I might be able to go back to
my country to bring aid to those women who need it. If the
country were at peace and a democracy and if they were to ask
me, I'd leave tomorrow to go and see how to organize the work
before settling there again for good. My children are grown and
would understand. Yes, that is my dearest wish.

Lyon, July 2001

In March 2001, I sent a letter to a young woman whom I had known
as a little girl in Kabul. Spoujmaï has grown and studied in communist Afghanistan. She became a doctor, got married, and had children.
Her brother told me that she writes extraordinary poems. She has
lived through all the stages that have marked Afghanistan in war and
still resides in Kabul today. Surely I wasn't going to get an answer.
How could she write me the story of her life? Where would she find
the time? She married a widower with five children, and she had
just given birth to her fourth child. She is a doctor at the hospital.

Her father was arrested when he was visiting her. The old man is condemned for his position during the communist regime. One could accumulate as many narratives as there are Afghan women, for each of their lives is a gold mine of information about the country. Unfortunately, that isn't possible and we will have to make do with what the press publishes every now and then—the story of a young girl, of a mother or a widow, an unrelenting repetition of the oppression they endure.

I met Chekeba Hachemi on March 21, 2001. The first day of spring, *Nawruz,* is also the first day of the Afghan year. Since that day, this young woman, with her frankness and her pure gaze, is the symbol of hope in the future of Afghanistan for me. Her account, like a profession of faith, will be a fitting conclusion to this book.

Chekeba is twenty-seven now and lives in Paris, where she arrived at the age of eleven. She has established an association whose goal it is wherever possible to help Afghans—men and women—reconstruct their country. She has absolutely no "false modesty." Her freedom of speech amazed me from the first time we met. She does not act any role, and she has fully come to terms with herself. Chekeba incorporates the best of both cultures, Afghan and French; she has the natural simplicity of those who do not doubt and have chosen to devote their lives to a cause.

She has created the association Free Afghanistan, and for two years now she has been going back to Afghanistan to bring the aid that will allow a dam to be constructed here, a school or a clinic elsewhere. Her idea is to be active in such a way that the Afghans will make the most of their abilities and stay in their country.

Chekeba Speaks, Paris, May 2001

I have a very good memory and I clearly remember my father's death when I was three years old. When the communist military coup d'état happened, I was four; I saw the tanks in Kabul, and I remember that we were all in the street to watch them go by.

There are twelve of us and I am the youngest. My mother had eleven children, one each year, and then there was a pause of six years before I was born. We're very neatly distributed: six boys and six girls. My father died, leaving my mother with all his children, half of whom still had to be raised.

My father, Sekandar Shah Hachemi, was an intellectual who came from a family of small landowners; he had worked hard, both at his studies and his first jobs, and succeeded in being promoted to a high position as civil servant in public works. He was also the governor of Herat and Kandahar, although he was from Kabul. He married my mother, who came from an upper-middle-class family of large retailers in the capital city. She attended school until she was about eleven or twelve, as was the custom then, and then she was taught at home by a tutor who was the instructor for a group of young girls in the family. She was fifteen when she was married. He chose her himself. He had been married before and had two children, but his wife had died. He was my uncle's best friend, and one day, when he came to visit him, he saw his sister. She was very pretty. Of course, she had noticed him as well, and it didn't take her long to say yes when he asked for her hand in marriage.

They loved each other very much, and my sisters tell me that he was actually deeply in love with her. Their arguments were fierce, as were their reconciliations. My mother always had a strong personality.

So, at the age of fifteen she settled down with my father in their own home. My father wanted to build his life by himself without having to depend on the family. He must have wanted to prove to his in-laws beyond a doubt that he could succeed on his own. That was a very modern way of being a couple in the Kabul of the fifties. The family increased year by year, and my father insisted on putting his children in the French lycées, Esteqlal for the boys and Malalaï for the girls. You shouldn't forget that the members of the royal family and of the entire Afghan elite sent their children to French schools at the time. They used to speak French fluently (a little like at the court of the czars in Russia), and many affluent young people would thereafter go and study at French universities. Furthermore, to a large extent France supported these lycées financially, from first grade through the final year of secondary school. For decades, thousands of children in Kabul learned French.

My father never went to France but always spoke of it with great feeling. He really was in love with that country and had told my mother that he dreamed of having one of his children speak French. That had an influence on us all, and half of us did come to France. You'll say that it was because of the war. But I can assure you that for us it was almost a challenge to succeed there. If only he could see us now! Just to speak of it gives me goose bumps. My father had high ambitions for his daughters: they were to go to the university and the question of their marrying was secondary. This shocked my mother, who used to answer that they first had to learn to run a home; in her eyes, becoming a mother was more important. His opinion differed radically from hers.

Professionally he was a success. He was, I believe, a man of integrity but also quite authoritarian. Still, everybody at home knew that my mother could get anything done from him. In spite of their age difference, she was the one who made the decisions. He was a demanding and strict father for his sons and especially kindhearted toward his daughters. He followed the boys' education closely and paid a lot of attention to their behavior. For my mother there were things that, socially speaking, could and could not be done. My father had moral standards that he wanted to instill in his children; he was a responsible educator and, among other things, insisted on his children showing respect to the people who worked for us. Besides, while my mother only had contact with people of her own milieu, he liked to be in touch with people different from himself—the farmers in Paghman, for example, which was the region where his family owned land. All this I have only been told and it must have influenced me. My father was one of those who had one ideal: he wanted to work for Afghanistan's development. And there isn't a day that goes by that I do not think of him.

Two weeks ago, a man from Panshir asked me if I was related to Sekandar Hachemi. I answered that he was my father. Then he said: "For me it is a point of pride to see that the man who did so much for the construction of Afghanistan has a daughter who today is speaking of the *reconstruction* of the country."

My mother liked receptions and the socialite life. She had the same dress designer as the queen and was very proud of that. My father adored my mother for her beauty and, undoubtedly, for her strong character as well, but he wasn't able to share his intellectual interests with her and for those he turned to his daughters. My oldest sister was married right after obtaining her bac, but after her studies in statistics the second one found a position in a ministerial department. The third one became a teacher. The fourth is a bank employee. The fifth one is a civil servant. And I am the sixth.

My oldest sister's wedding apparently caused a calamity at home. My mother had arranged the marriage, and my father didn't agree. On the photos you can see he looks absolutely furious! My second sister fell in love with the head of her department; he was an Uzbek who had gone to the United States to study and upon his return was appointed head of his department at the Ministry of Social Affairs. His family, who lived in the northwest, barely spoke Persian; he was very bright. My father was the one who organized that marriage, the ceremony, and paid all the costs, wanting to show that he accepted him as a son. He was especially proud of this particular son-in-law. The boy actually had somewhat of a similar history as he himself did, having on his own merits risen to an important place. They now live in New York, where both of them are civil servants.

All the daughters are married with the exception of myself. One is in Germany, two others are in Holland, and the one who is a teacher is still in Pakistan. She fled Kabul with her five daughters and one son when the Taliban came in. Her husband, who used to work in a bank in Kabul, no longer does anything. She is very courageous. When they arrived in Pakistan, she found a job as a manual laborer right away and then she started teaching Persian to Pakistanis and set up courses in hygiene for a group of Afghan women. She is waiting for the Taliban to leave so that she can go back home. Her older children have emigrated to the United States. The three younger ones are with her.

My six brothers live in France. The oldest one met his wife, who is French, while working as a guide for an Afghan tourist agency. They have a twenty-year-old son and a nineteen-year-old daughter and are now living in Paris. The second one earned a scholarship from the French government. The other brothers did their studies with the war going on and the risk of being drafted into the army.

My mother didn't want to leave. The danger was there for her sons, and she made sure they left one by one. But my brothers in Europe became more and more deeply involved in the resistance, and since they were afraid for us, they insisted that she make a decision. The youngest one, who is six years older than I, was still in Kabul. My mother had private means and no financial problems. But she shouldn't sell anything to prepare for her departure in order not to attract attention and be exposed. She made her decision and one night we left. My youngest brother had gone to Pakistan just one week ahead of us.

They brought us to Jalalabad by car, where we stayed for four days with the person who was helping us out and where we were forbidden to wash so that we would lose our urban look and take on the guise of Pashtun peasants. My mother was asthmatic, it was February, and I was eleven years old. The smuggler told us that if we were stopped at a checkpoint we shouldn't talk or say that we were together. We were in the bus that was supposed to take us to Peshawar; my mother sat next to one smuggler, I next to another and two young women who made the trip regularly for business reasons. I had almost never left Kabul and had just spent four days with this family in which everyone spoke Pashtun and I had been turned into a little farm girl. At the first checkpoint, the soldiers interrogated the passengers and asked the man I was with who I was. He answered, "A young Pashtun girl who is going to her family in Peshawar." The majority of the people in Peshawar are Pashtun, and their comings and goings from one side or the other of the border don't arouse any suspicion from the military. Next to the soldier was a Russian woman who then gave me a big smile to which I couldn't help but respond. One Afghan soldier immediately reacted: "She isn't Pashtun, she's city girl!" A peasant girl would never have smiled at a stranger! The smuggler came out of the bus with me. I can still see my mother as in a movie: I was moving away and she looked at me, totally distraught, but couldn't do anything, for that would have caused us all to be lost. The smuggler in charge of her held her arms so she wouldn't make any gestures. The two women had also been arrested. We waited. The soldiers had gone off a little way. Suddenly, the smuggler said to us: "I'm going to count to three and then you'll run to that brook over there. Even if you hear any shots, don't move, just wait for me there." It was full daylight. We ran and I got tangled up in my big clothes with some sort of thongs on my feet. But I dashed off with the others. I don't remember any shooting, but I've been told that the soldiers did fire. The bus had gone on already, taking my mother away, and I was alone with people I didn't know. I now believe that the smuggler must have arranged things by paying the soldiers, which is quite possible. It should be known that half of the passage was paid before departing and that the man in question wouldn't get the rest until arrival in Peshawar. Fleeing people are important merchandise for the smugglers.

We waited for nightfall and no one came to bother us; then we left and had to walk for a week. We would sleep in villages, in barns of a sort. The following day, as we came to a stable where there were two other men whom the smuggler knew, I tried to get closer to the women, of course, but it was each for herself. I asked questions but to no avail. I was crying and asking where my mother was and when we would arrive. Nobody would talk to me. The next day, we walked and hid from the helicopters beneath our huge black veils; I couldn't stop crying and stumbling because of the thongs. The others didn't slow down to wait for me, and when we came to a camp of nomads that was our stop for the night, the smuggler said to me: "I couldn't care less if you don't want to keep up with us, I'll tell them in Peshawar that you died in a helicopter attack; those things happen and you have nothing to say about it. I could even sell you right here: I'm sure to find a buyer for a young girl from Kabul." He had no compassion whatsoever, nor did the women. Perhaps he even believed what he was saying—we'd heard these things happened to girls on the road. Did he say this to scare me and force me to move faster? I tend to think, though, that the women and he were all totally blasé: they had helped thousands of people under these conditions across for money and were no longer aware that their merchandise was human beings. Today, when I'm asked what scares me, I answer, "Nothing!" I always see myself there that night, sitting on the straw, hating that man intensely, and my reaction was to decide that that crook would never again have the satisfaction of seeing my weakness. That is where my will was born. I was watching the two women sleeping, completely indifferent. I told myself I would never, ever cry again. In one night I became a grown-up.

We moved on the next morning. I hardly ate anything because the food was disgusting to the little spoiled city girl I was. I feel a bit ashamed when I think of it, but the smell of goats, the filth, it was all new to me. My pride took over from all the rest, and I followed them with clenched teeth until we arrived. At night I'd cry all by myself, but during the day I held up. On the road we'd meet groups of resisters. Mountains followed upon mountains—it was interminable. My attitude may have forced them to respect me; in any event, they left me in peace. On the last day they even sat me on a bony donkey to finish the trip.

No one knew what had become of me. And yet, the smugglers are well organized, since as soon as we arrived in the tribal zone[4] a jeep came to get us and take us to Peshawar.

I threw myself into the arms of my mother, who had been waiting for a week, together with my brother. Friends took us in. My other brothers had prepared everything for our journey to France. Two of them had been naturalized and thus had no trouble getting us to come three weeks later.

In the plane, my head was bubbling over and I was making my mother crazy with my plans. When we arrived at Orly my

---

[4]The buffer zone between Pakistan and Afghanistan.

brothers were waiting for us, and it was a unique moment of
happiness for us all. It was raining, it was April, but I was in
heaven. My brother's children and his French wife were there.
All I could say was "bonjour" and "au revoir," but words don't
matter at moments like that.

Until I was eleven, my life had been rather carefree, highly
protected by my family, whereas the Soviet occupation had a
dramatic influence on the lives of those adults who had traveled
before. As for me, I continued to go to school and to live in a
limited universe, quite large enough for me.

The lycée was very close to the house. We lived in a new
district of Kabul and all my friends lived there as well. We
would go to the movies and eat ice cream. My sisters wore
jeans. I could sense that serious things were happening: adults
would gather at the house and have long discussions; people
from the countryside used to come by, and I'd hear bits of
information concerning imprisonment and war. But they
kept the little girl I was removed from all that; we played the
usual games that Afghan children play, poetry competitions at
recreation time, for instance. We used to learn many poems.
All the ones I know today I learned before I was eleven: Hafiz,
Nezami, Rumi . . . We were divided into two groups: the first
would start a poem, the second had to pick up from the last
syllable and recite another poem, and so on. The group that
lost inspiration would lose the match. We played this at home
also. I began school when I was five and was the youngest, so I
learned a great deal from the older ones. My sister used to read
me her fiancé's letters and took me into her confidence when I
was nine years old. When she married a year later, it broke my
heart. Today she is in Germany. When I was little, my brothers
and sisters actually paid more attention to me than my mother
did. I began to feel the tension caused by the war when my
brothers left. The teachers at school who were Communists

wanted to recruit me into one of the youth movements and my mother began to be afraid for me. The French courses at the lycée had been replaced with courses in Russian.

The day I arrived in France, I told the sister-in-law with whom we were staying that I wanted to start school the next day. She was a teacher in a middle school and took me there.

That April, I went to seventh grade just for the last trimester! I didn't understand a word. This was in Châtenay-Malabry, and I was the only foreign child. I remember that all the other kids were trying to teach me dirty words by having me repeat after them. I changed schools when the new school year began and was registered for eighth grade. Not only had I not mastered French yet, but I had to learn English, too. They helped me at home, but improving quickly was a challenge for me. I knew the alphabet and skimmed books without being able to decipher a single word. I watched, listened, and registered everything with unbelievable eagerness. I spoke French with my nephews, who were four and five, and, living with the sister-in-law who spoke no Persian, I was immersed in a French-speaking world. My hunger for learning helped me overcome every obstacle.

This sister-in-law became like a second mother to me. My teachers from that period, surprised at my development, helped me enormously as well. By the end of eighth grade I had caught up with the other students. In ninth grade I was among the best in the school, and in the end I received my bac with honors. I used to devour books. My sister-in-law raised me like a French girl and I always had many friends among the boys.

My brothers wanted to help me choose a profession. I was actually very independent and told them to get lost. Today they want to protect me, all the while admiring the choice I made and my commitment. They are also a bit afraid of what I am. I am a mystery to them because I affirm my freedom. I intrigue them because I get along very well with their wives, who confide in me. It bothers them that I am aware of their innermost feelings. Four of them are married to French women. My best Afghan friend married my youngest brother. We are very close.

From the very start, I wanted to be a doctor and go to Afghanistan. I was growing up in a circle of people who were helping the resistance and who continued to be very concerned by what was going on there. Working for my father's country has always been so obvious to me: it was my country and I should make myself useful to it. I wanted to be a "Doctor without Borders." In my first year of premed I realized that physics was something I didn't understand, while I was very good in economics and letters. My sister-in-law made me accept the fact that doctors aren't the only ones who can contribute something to a country that is at war, like Afghanistan.

I have always had an intense personality. When I was very young, I saw a documentary on female excision that revolted me, and I wanted to go to Africa to fight this scourge. Passionate to prove that an Afghan woman could succeed brilliantly, I decided to study economics and business. I didn't apply for French citizenship until I had started a business, thereby proving that I was "up to their level." It was as if my father were watching me at every stage of my life; I feel his presence by my side. I grew up with the pride of knowing what he was and I want to be worthy of being his daughter. So when I go there to provide some assistance it is very emotional when I meet someone who used to know him.

At the student office of the business school where I studied, I suggested that we organize evenings to raise funds for Afghanistan, and in 1994 three friends of mine and I created an association whose primary goal is aid for the reconstruction of schools. In 2000, I went to the territories that were not under Taliban control to bring them the equivalent of the annual salary of primary school teachers. I realized that it was, indeed, possible to aid the economic development by financing, as we did that year, the construction of a small dam to produce electricity. But what is even more important than money is the encounter.

The men and women who fled the war and the dictatorship imposed by the Taliban, those who wanted to shelter their wives and daughters from an obscurantist regime, all need to know that they are not being abandoned.

I admire Massoud, the leader of the Panshir, because even during the war against the Communists he tried to organize life in the villages by concentrating specifically on the education of children. Sometimes they ask me here what construction is good for if war destroys everything the next day. If everybody had been reasoning that way for twenty-three years, there would be nothing and nobody alive in Afghanistan. Today we have to fight so that those who didn't leave and who have abilities can work on-site.

We know that once you have been forced to leave your country, it is painful to think back on it, and some people, in despair after the events, are tempted to turn the page. For me, on the other hand, it is gratifying to work for my country, to sensitize people who otherwise would never have known Afghanistan. We need every strength and force available to overcome these difficult times. Relying on my behavior and my freedom of tone, some people have told me that I've become completely French. I always answer that if I have become so fully integrated it is because I have held on to my roots.

I am Afghan, solidly anchored in my culture and my religion, which is where I get my energy. And when I mention Afghanistan, I don't do so as a European feminist because I know that one should adapt one's speech to those one talks with. And every time I am surprised again by the receptivity of the

Afghans I meet there. They are eager for peace and progress, and thus ready to accept newness in their lives. You shouldn't hurt their feelings, and to that end all that is sometimes needed is to observe the proper form. Unfortunately, when Afghanistan is mentioned people often stop at the conventional issues: "Suppress the chador, which is intolerable, and perhaps there will be some hope for progress in the country." Yes, it is intolerable, but it doesn't bother me if, in order not to shock many women as well as men, I must wear a veil to be able to discuss opening a school for girls or a department of gynecology. With a veil on her head, no Afghan woman has ever stopped herself from letting her voice be heard, and frequently it is she who has the last word. A change in the status of women cannot be obtained that fast. One should always put oneself within the context if one wants to be effective. I choose efficiency over polemics.

Until last year I had a job and was able to dedicate only my spare time to getting people to know and help Afghanistan. But when I sensed how much the people I met there were beginning to depend on me, I became aware that I was the intermediary between their suffering and the hope they are placing in the West. That is quite a responsibility. It was my first contact with rural and poor Afghanistan, a far remove from my own social milieu, and yet communicating has been very easy. I didn't know how the people would take me: as a French woman or as someone like them? Well, rapport was established without any difficulty. Afghans, even the illiterate, are extraordinarily open-minded, and you can speak very candidly with both men and women.

I met Commander Massoud during my first trip. Like everyone in France, I found him physically attractive and rather pleasant, but I had no political tie whatsoever with his party. I don't have one today either, but I must acknowledge that his sincerity and his modesty convinced me he was a decent man.

Besides, he was the only one who didn't abandon his country. After 1996, he was alone with just a handful of men against the Taliban. When communism fell, he wasn't able to hold on to power, but let's not forget that the other resistance parties didn't give him a thing and that he had to confront a general civil war.

When I asked him why we couldn't meet his wife, he simply answered, "It's a question of security." That is why there are no photographs at all of his wife and children. It was Massoud who told me that young Westernized Afghans like myself could be of incomparable help to the country if they would emulate some of the French who have been going there since the beginning of the war, working in clinics, schools, or improving agricultural development projects.

My generation has a sense of the concrete. We aren't victims of nostalgia since we haven't known the Afghanistan of my parents. We have everything to learn, and we can bring them what we have been taught in the West. Because of that, perhaps we are stronger. For me that is where hope lies, in this new generation that will be enticed, as some of the French are, by the charm of the country and by the awareness that we can be useful to a people that expects everything from us. For example, there are Afghan women doctors in exile who could come and practice in the existing clinics and hospitals. There are agronomists and teachers. In the West we have a whole breeding ground of competent people who would live a much happier life if they could feel they were useful to their country. Sometimes it is enough to give a bit of an example to prove this is possible.

The subject of the Afghan woman is a delicate topic. Officially, it was at the root of the failure of King Amanullah's modernization policy, then that of the Communists. The essence lies in educating girls. I have studied, and thanks to that I can vie with my brothers in any discussion that comes up. Had I not been educated, I wouldn't know my religion about which I have read books in several languages. Today, if you introduce yourself as someone who has come to teach a lesson, speaking of the rights that should be granted to Afghan women and holding forth with feminist talk that scares them, the men close up. But if you mention their daughters' education, they are wholly prepared to accept our reasoning and they themselves will ask for it. Being an Afghan woman is a priceless trump card, because for me there are no taboos: I can use the informal *you* form when referring to "your wife" or "your daughters" without being impolite. Paradoxically, men have many more subjects they cannot talk about than we do; in fact, it has always struck me how much freedom of expression women have.

In contrast to generally accepted ideas, the people I met in the country itself are not passive or numbed by poverty. I am touched by their dignity, by the fact that they speak of the future. Farmers' wives who have lost their sons look at me with shining eyes: "You are our future Benazir Bhutto!" The woman who said that to me had never been out of her village, but her spirit soared beyond the mountains.

Several million Afghans died or fled their country, but there is a large number left who have truly open minds and technical know-how. Everything should be done to keep these valuable people and have them stay there and be able to live off their work. They should be given something concrete to accomplish, and their children should be able to study. With a minimum of means, they will mobilize and feel life coming back to them.

If we wait to act until the war is over it will be too late.

And don't let them come and tell me that I'm sacrificing myself for this cause. I'm getting something out of it because it is wonderful to see the effect of the smallest gesture one makes toward those who have such high hopes of us.

Chekeba, upon Returning from Afghanistan, August 28, 2001

I left France on July thirty-first and came back on the fourteenth of August, having thus spent two weeks in the Panshir Valley.

I went there to launch the building of a new Lycée Malalaï, a school for girls where we want English and French courses to be taught. We brought the funds to begin the construction of the buildings, and I must now find financing to get the school up and running. It could open its doors when the new school year begins on March 21, 2002. They ask me whether I'm not afraid that the plan won't come to fruition, but I keep thinking that if I wait to get the whole budget together nothing will ever happen. The buildings of the lycée alone should cost $80,000 and we estimate the annual budget to be $30,000. This is for a thousand students with twelve classes from elementary to the last year of secondary school.

It will be the second lycée in the Panshir Valley. The first one is too small to take in girls after they finish primary school. The level of the teachers is very low, and our project includes the creation of a department of teacher training that we can have come from Kabul. Today, quite a few of them are hesitant to come to the free zones for fear of not finding any work there.

We welcome everyone into the association, men and women, who want to help in the reconstruction of our country, with priority for actions on behalf of women; but the suffering of men equals that of women, and we would like the "Afghan problem" not to be reduced to a "problem of Afghan women and the chador." We don't provide emergency aid, but we devote ourselves to reconstruction by starting with the foundations of a society: let the children be educated and let the adults have work.

I brought members of a Swiss association along with me to start an orphanage in the valley. We rented a house and then found three or four local women, widows who were living in the village. We asked every NGO there to draw up a list of orphans and send them to us. The women are paid, and afternoon courses are organized so that the children become at least literate. It is an opportunity to prove that small structures can be created that provide work for people without any resources. It's still very limited, but the impetus has been given. Our permanent concern is proving that we can count on the locals to reorganize society.

Back in Europe, I can show that the projects to be financed are quite concrete. The principle of our operation is to place the first stone and then present the plans to continue the work. Otherwise enormous amounts of time are wasted and the situation only gets worse.

During this trip I also went to the region of Sharikar, where I found Madame Zara, the former principal of the Lycée Zarghuna, a large girls' lycée in Kabul that was shut down when the Taliban came into the capital. This woman did not want to leave the country, even though all her children emigrated because of the war. So she stayed loyal to her post until there was really no way anymore for her to do anything. We get along famously since both of us think that one should act on the spot, right there in Afghanistan.

I met her for the first time last spring, when she had organized a Woman's Day, and thereafter she sent me several letters telling me she was short of money; I suggested that I would help her create a women's cooperative in the town where she lives.

She counted almost eight hundred women, the majority of whom are widows, for whom we want to establish workshops in embroidery, dressmaking, apprenticeships in foreign language learning, teacher training, and so on. Our goal is for the cooperative to be self-sufficient financially at the end of the first year. While we wait, we need help in positioning the infrastructure and purchasing the materials. All that still needs to be put into place, but the ideas grow as we discuss them.

If an Afghan woman is given work, it is the opportunity for her to bring home a salary and thereby acquire greater authority. It is not by staying within four walls, totally dependent upon her husband financially, that a woman can command respect for what she says. It serves absolutely no purpose to talk to women about their rights if they cannot even understand what it's all about.

For instance, during this last trip I came to the conclusion that most women know nothing about maternal and child protection. Many of them have never been outside of their village, they have too many children, and they have gynecological problems that nobody is taking care of; they terminate pregnancies by whatever means they have, which leads to dramas we all know. Therefore we must create centers for family planning. We have spoken with the women, their husbands, and even with two mullahs to whom I posed the question and who responded by saying that it was necessary to prevent all births under the present situation of adversity. "It goes against Islam," they told me, "to bring children into the world whom you cannot feed." The establishment of a clinic for family planning in the Panshir Valley requires the presence of a female physician specialist who could train and organize teams. Whether she stays three or six months, it would be enough to get the work started.

What struck the journalists who were with me the most was the difference that exists between cities and rural areas. In the country, people haven't changed; they haven't undergone the influences of the successive political regimes. Royalty, republics, communist regime, the Taliban—their life grows a little more wretched every year but remains everywhere the same.

Afghan culture is still there, it is the culture of the countryside. The only chance to make women's condition evolve is to offer them an education. By building the large Lycée Malalaï in the Panshir, we're proving that we're not working for something temporary, and it is a symbol of hope.

We want to encourage initiatives in the villages. In Afghanistan, there is a village culture, and if you create something that starts in the village it has every chance of succeeding. Fathers will more readily accept their daughters' going to school if the school is close to home.

Young educated girls we met told us: "The only difference between my mother and myself is that I'll be capable of answering my husband." Society evolves. The reputation of the Taliban is such that education has become a goal for families to attain.

We must take one step at a time. Not burning one's bridges. It should proceed in such a way that the request comes naturally; and since there are many urban people who took refuge in the country, the need for schools is obvious to them.

A school is the first thing they ask for when we visit a village. People are hungry, have no health care, but their first wish is for their children to be educated.

I saw Massoud again and spoke with him about the condition of Afghan women, telling him that Taliban or not, the situation of women preoccupies me a great deal. He answered: "Since time immemorial, women in Afghanistan wear chains around their ankles. On the one hand, under the Taliban regime, these chains are tightened and made heavier, on the other we try to undo them by taking away one link after another. Confronted with the customs of each region, we cannot afford to take the chains off in one fell swoop." We talked a great deal about the fact that certain things are shocking to us, such as wearing the chador. He told me that if some women of the Panshir had begun to wear the chador it was under the influence of the city women: "If I prohibit the chador in the valley, I will be acting like the Taliban but in reverse; that is not the important point. What counts is that boys and girls be educated and then the chador will disappear by itself."

For the first time I had a long conversation with Massoud's wife, whom I had met a year earlier in Tajikistan. She is the daughter of one of Massoud's aides-de-camp, the first one to have received him in the valley when the Soviets invaded. Massoud came from a Kabul family, originally from the Panshir, of middle-class intellectuals. He didn't want to get married, but from a certain age on it is not well looked upon to be a bachelor, even for a commander. Some wanted him to marry an intellectual, but he preferred taking the young daughter of the house, thereby showing his gratitude to his aide-de-camp and his family. She was seventeen.

She had a terrible life, first spending her entire childhood in the holes made to hide from the bombings, a life that consisted of fleeing from war for more than twenty years, and seeing her aunt torn to shreds in childbirth by a bomb; cold and hunger. The commander was her idol, and one can imagine her joy when they came to ask for her in marriage on his behalf. The ceremony took place in secret, and the day after the wedding, as the bombings went on incessantly, her husband disappeared for six months; since then, she cannot have spent more than two days straight with him. She lives in Tajikistan with her children, for as soon as she spends a few days in the Panshir there is an attack by the Taliban; people die and are wounded. They try to attack her, and it is others who are bombed.

She has a boy of eleven and five girls. The oldest of the little girls says that she wants to be a journalist and another wants to be a doctor. Their father looks at them with a tender gaze and tells me that perhaps they should study at a foreign university.

She receives women, some thirty or so a day, who come to

bring her lists of grievances and ask for her help; when she sees her husband again, a good deal of her time is taken up playing the role of messenger.

She, too, stressed the importance of creating a clinic for family planning in the valley, for she told us she felt powerless to help the women who came to see her with serious gynecological problems.

She has large green eyes and a dazzling smile, and she recounts all of this quite simply and gently. She is full of admiration for her husband. He spends all the time he possibly can with his daughters, helping them with their homework. She proudly showed me the library they have gradually collected; he helped her become more cultured and she loves to read the Persian poets. It was somewhat of an ideal family, in spite of the insecurity caused by the political situation and even with the war that separated them, sometimes for more than a year.

When the Communists left Kabul and the resistance took the capital, the bombings by the opposing factions began immediately, and she had to leave with her children to live in a camp outside the city.

Recently, and this explains the library's presence, the inhabitants of the valley built a house for her and her children with a nice garden. Her first real home. Do they feel more secure? Who knows? She told me she hadn't been made to wear the chador yet since she has never gone out of the house unless she was escorted. She accepts this life, out of love.

Today, I am returning to Europe with confidence in the future. I know whom I can count on in Afghanistan. I have concrete projects on which to work, and I would like to be able to go back there every two or three months. The welcome is so amazing and I feel comfortable there.

I also do political work in Europe, because this situation could go on for years if we don't intervene to prevent the

Pakistanis from destabilizing Afghanistan. We don't yet dare call things by their name: it is a foreign invasion. The military are Pakistanis or come from Arab countries. Sympathy for the lot of women is inadequate if we do nothing to liberate the country. We need to look at the long term.

Pakistan is an important client of the French weapons factories. France is presumably the third-largest provider of arms to Pakistan. It was the French, after all, who sold the nuclear reactor recently installed in Pakistan.

When I was speaking of the construction of a girls' lycée in the Panshir Valley, an adviser to the French cabinet asked me to call upon French architects so that the buildings would be "up to standard." Before even listening to our presentation of the project and giving any thought to helping us!

Last week, the representative of a European Ministry of Foreign Affairs asked me if there wasn't a great deal of propaganda attached to the unpleasant information circulating about the Taliban. It makes you believe they don't want to think . . .

When Kabul women in chadors testify before the assembly of deputies, they are given an ovation and everyone agrees that "it's horrible," but two months later they begin to wonder whether it is not "exaggerated." You have to be mentally strong to keep going.

Pakistan depends entirely on the economic aid of the West, which should be able to pressure this powerful neighbor to abandon its claims on our country.

In France I count on a few people who are convinced of our integrity and the value of our struggle. We are practicing politics but outside the parties. In the fall, women of the French Senate are going to accompany me to the Panshir to evaluate the situation. All parties together. I do not belong to Massoud's party even if I admire his charisma and his path on which he himself recognizes having made some mistakes.

I have no political solution whatsoever for my country. It is up to the Afghans to decide their destiny. Massoud is the only one who continues to bring men together to resist the barbarism. That doesn't mean that he will be leading Afghanistan tomorrow. Pockets of resistance are forming here and there. My goal is to be able to intervene everywhere it's possible to create structures that will allow children to be educated and adults to rebuild their lives.

The life we used to lead in Kabul before the war, in the privileged milieu from which I came, was that of barely 2 percent of the population. Many of us, who had the means left Kabul, quite simply because it had become impossible to have a decent life there. But there are all the other Afghan men and women who remain: those who fled by the thousands into camps where they are surviving wretchedly, holding on to the hope of going home one day; they are the ones who can't or won't leave their country.

It for them that I am fighting.

Massoud had told Chekeba that he wanted to liberate the women from their chains, link by link. Massoud is no longer, but Chekeba will not be the only one to continue the struggle.

September 24, 2001

Chekeba went back again to Afghanistan. The Panshir Valley was besieged by journalists, but the young woman was able to complete her mission: "Life goes on," she says. "We have to bring our projects to a close; the large girls' lycée, the Lycée Malalaï of the Panshir, is under construction; we expect to have a section for teacher training there. The Nawalige Dam, which we financed, produces electricity today. We opened a primary school in Qalatsha for a hundred and thirty little girls, in collaboration with the mullah and prominent villagers. The women's cooperative of Gulbahar is taking shape.

From the start, the reason for our association has been the reconstruction of the country by offering Afghan men and women jobs on the spot that match their abilities; that is what we will continue to do tomorrow in every region of Afghanistan."

November 13, 2001

The Afghans are very pleased with the happy turn events were taking. Will they know how to take advantage of the unique chance that is being given them to rebuild their country thanks to the financial and logistical support of rich countries? Individually, Afghans have shown a great capacity for adaptation both in exile and in war.

Let us send them our wishes for reconstruction and advancement on the path to progress, a progress that will take their cultural wealth and their specificity into account; a progress that will be possible only by using every strength of the country, including that of the Afghan women.

Besides having lived and taught in Afghanistan for four years (1974–1978), **Isabelle Delloye** has traveled extensively, living and working in Tunisia, Nicaragua, Pakistan, and the United States. She now lives in Paris, where she is on the board of a humanitarian association called Afghanistan Libre (Free Afghanistan). She lectures extensively in France on the subject of Afghan women, seeking active and financial support for the many development projects being implemented on behalf of the people she loves.

Marjolijn de Jager is an award-winning translator from the French and Dutch, with special interests in francophone African literature and women writers. She currently teaches literary translation at New York University, as well as French and Dutch language courses.